W9-ARR-537

# About the Cover

The image on the cover is an ancient glyph that stands for transcendence. The symbol typically has a white line that runs across the top of the triangle, but I put in a red line instead. Why? The red line signifies the unconventional winning approach I describe in **Brands Don't Win**. I call this modified symbol the "Transcender System Triangle." Throughout the book, I will fill in this Triangle with the three proven, practical steps of The Transcender System™ that inspire leading companies to transcend traditional brand competitors to win.

# BRANDS DON'T WIN

# BRANDS DON'T WIN

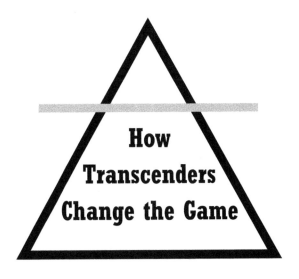

How
Transcenders
Change the Game

## Stan Bernard, MD, MBA

LIONCREST
PUBLISHING

BRANDS DON'T WIN
*How Transcenders Change the Game*

ISBN   978-1-5445-2232-6  *Hardcover*
          978-1-5445-2231-9  *Paperback*
          978-1-5445-2230-2  *Ebook*
          978-1-5445-2233-3  *Audiobook*

*Dedication: To my father, who always inspires me to help others win...*

# Contents

## INTRODUCTION

Introduction: How Winners Win.............................. 13

1. The Transcender Revolution .................................21

2. Winning with a Political Playbook ....................... 33
   *Barack Obama's 2008 Presidential Campaign*

## STEP I: CREATE THE AGENDA

3. Play Your Game ........................................................53

4. The Three Techniques to Create the Agenda ......... 65
   *Apple*

5. Competitive Creation............................................... 77
   *Starbucks*

6. Competitive Re-Creation ....................................... 87
   *Peloton*

7. Competitive Categorization ...................................95
   *Seedlip*
   *Uber*

## STEP II: COMMUNICATE THE AGENDA

8. **Memorable** ..................................................111
GEICO

9. **Ownable** .................................................. 127
Sweetgreen

10. **Winnable** .................................................. 135
Nike

11. **Alignable** .................................................. 143
Amazon

## STEP III: CHAMPION THE AGENDA

12. **Access** .................................................. 155
Google
Zara

13. **Advantages** .......................................... 167
Tesla

14. **Advangelicals** ....................................... 179
Lemi Shine
Glossier

15. **Awareness** .......................................... 197
Halo Top
Carrie Hammer

## CONCLUSION

16. **Applying the Transcender System** ....................... 211

**About the Author** .................................. 223

**Acknowledgments** ................................ 225

**Glossary** ............................................ 229

**Bibliography** ...................................... 235

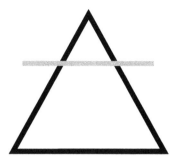

# INTRODUCTION

# Introduction

## HOW WINNERS WIN

On October 4, 1957, the Soviet Union stunned the United States and the world by launching the first satellite, Sputnik I, into orbit. This feat suggested that the USSR had made a quantum leap forward in technology, which posed a serious threat to US national security. Would the USSR attack the United States with the same powerful rockets that had propelled Sputnik into orbit? The United States was so shocked by this historic event that the phrase "Sputnik Moment" has come to mean a point in time when a competitor recognizes it is falling behind its rival.

The Sputnik launch was a microcosm of the much larger Cold War being waged by the world's two most powerful nations. The Cold War pitted the Soviet Union against the United States in an ideological, political, economic, technological, and military struggle for dominant world influence. Each was eager to push its global agenda: communism for the Soviet Union and democracy for the United States. Literally and figuratively, the highest form of competition between these two rivals was the so-called Space Race from 1955–1969.

Four years after Sputnik, the United States was blindsided again when the Soviet Union's cosmonaut Yuri Gagarin orbited the Earth in the Vostok 1 capsule. This event sent shockwaves and alarms through the United States. President John F. Kennedy and his cabinet understood that their nation was in fear of a potential Soviet missile attack from space. Kennedy knew the United States could not win this Space Race; the USSR had already won by launching the first satellite and the first human into orbit. Kennedy decided to *change the game* from the Space Race to the Moon Race. And he did it with four words: "Man on the Moon."

On May 25, 1961, Kennedy recommended to Congress that the United States "should commit itself to achieving the goal, before this decade is out, of landing a man on the Moon and returning him safely to the Earth." He again proclaimed this goal to Americans and to the world in a speech on September 12, 1962, in Houston: "This nation should commit itself to achieving the goal, before this decade is out, of landing a man on the Moon and returning him safely to the Earth… We choose to go to the Moon…because that challenge is one that we intend to win."

Kennedy changed the "space game" by changing the measure by which the world would evaluate the two superpowers: the winning measure was not the "first man into space" but the "first man on the Moon." He had moved the proverbial goal posts.

The day before his speech in 1962, Kennedy visited NASA in Houston for the first time. As the story goes, Kennedy saw a man in the hallway carrying a broom. "What do you do for NASA?" Kennedy asked. "I'm helping put a man on the Moon," the janitor responded. This janitor understood the greater purpose of his role because of Kennedy's 1961 speech. If he did his job cleaning and taking out the trash, he would enable NASA's scientists, engineers, and astronauts to focus their time on their mission of putting a man on the Moon.

Kennedy changed the agenda from the Soviet Space Race to the US Man on the Moon with several winning Actions. He obtained an additional $9 billion in funding for NASA's mission and ensured access to the nation's best engineers, scientists, and technologies, including IBM's cutting-edge computing system.

Tragically, John F. Kennedy was assassinated on November 22, 1963, and never had the chance to see a man on the Moon. However, Kennedy's lunar mission was fulfilled by his dedicated NASA team. On July 20, 1969, US astronaut Neil Armstrong became the first man on the Moon.

In its 2019 report *Iconic Moves: Transforming Customer Expectations*, the consulting firm Interbrand reflected on the role that Kennedy's concise wording played in this unprecedented achievement. They interviewed Apollo 11 crew member Michael Collins, who spoke of Kennedy's commitment as a "powerful driving force for the mission's success." He said, "*The single-mindedness and clarity of that statement [the 1961 speech] worked as a true north throughout the years leading to the mission—helping overcome obstacles, speeding up processes, and providing everyone with a clear goal and timeline... The simplicity, the stark beauty of John Kennedy's mandate...really helped us along to the Moon.*"

Kennedy and the US won the Space Race by "changing the game" to the race to the Moon. This approach of changing the game is commonly used by politicians, especially during elections. Politicians call it "Changing the Agenda." In political terms, a "Campaign Agenda" is the core, overarching concept that a candidate wants to convey to constituents—as well as the game the candidate forces his rivals to play. Kennedy's concise, four-word Campaign Agenda of "Man on the Moon" and his supporting actions led to one of mankind's greatest historical feats.

As a global competition consultant for over 35 years, I have found that leading companies also change the game with Campaign Agendas, *not branding*. Historically, conventional companies have primarily differentiated their brands by using marketing tactics. However, businesses like Apple, Starbucks, and Peloton have not played the traditional brand game; they have created their *own* game, executed their Agenda, and forced competitors to play by their rules.

In 1997, Apple was on the verge of bankruptcy before Steve Jobs propelled the company to become the world's most valuable with his two-word Campaign Agenda of "Think Different." Jeff Bezos led Amazon to become the earth's dominant retailer by implementing his two-word Campaign Agenda of "Customer Obsession." Starbucks went from adding one store per year to nearly four stores *per day* by executing a three-word Agenda, "The Third Place," that transformed the global coffee business.

In just four years, Seedlip was able to dominate the non-alcoholic spirits category by playing an entirely new game. Peloton re-created the world-class studio cycling experience, while tiny Halo Top Ice Cream surpassed brand behemoth Unilever with its "Guilt-Free Ice Cream" game. Many other companies—including Google, Uber, Glossier, and Sweet-green—have also changed the game to win in their markets. I call these companies "Transcenders" because they have risen above their conventional competitors by using more of a political playbook than a product playbook.

When I was a young sports fan, I was obsessed with finding an answer to a single question: why do some teams win, and others lose? I wondered how Alabama's Crimson Tide football team would pummel my beloved Vanderbilt Commodores every year—the game was typically over by the second quarter. That was when I first realized that Alabama's legendary coach Paul "Bear" Bryant had a *winning system*, heavily focused on better player recruiting and development.

Around the same time, I watched and marveled at how Coach John Wooden was guiding his UCLA Bruins to 88 straight wins—the longest stretch in men's college basketball history—on his way to 10 NCAA titles in 12 years. I discovered that he won using his 15-block winning system called the "Pyramid of Success." I would spend hours studying and analyzing games to understand how these and other legendary teams won so consistently.

As I got older, Alabama's dominance over Vanderbilt—and most other teams—continued. 'Bama has won 36 of the last 37 games against Vanderbilt, with the most recent victories coming under the leadership of renowned coach Nick Saban. In 2020, Saban surpassed Bear Bryant for the most college football championships because he, like Bryant, has a winning system. He calls it "The Process," which focuses not on results, but on the factors that lead to those results: superior player identification, recruitment, development, practice, and game preparation. He adopted part of his system from his former coach and mentor, New England Patriots coach Bill Belichick. Belichick has won a record six National Football League Super Bowls by applying his "Do Your Job" winning system.

When I began to take more of an interest in business, I saw there was a "game" in business too—with clear winners and losers. With the same determination that I'd had with teams, I set out to study businesses to understand that game and how to win it.

As a business executive and consultant, I spent decades searching for a winning system for business, but no one and no book could quite explain why some businesses win and others lose. So, I decided to *create* a winning system.

My aha moment came during Senator Barack Obama's presidential election campaign in 2008. I was captivated by the brilliant campaign communications and strategies that this little-known, first-term Senator used to beat two well-known political rivals: Hillary Clinton, to win the Democratic nomination, and John McCain, to win the Presidency. Obama's agenda driven approach was similar to how certain companies, like Amazon and Apple, have *transcended* so far above their competitors. I named my campaign-style approach the "Transcender System™."

**The Transcender System is a powerful, proven, and practical approach that all business professionals can learn and apply to help their company win.** I have tested this system's effectiveness through my consulting engagements with over a dozen Fortune 500 companies and 150 other companies, across 60 countries spanning six continents and involving over 15,000 business professionals. The Transcender System consistently works because it forces competitors to play your company's game—a game only your company can win.

For 14 years, I taught the Transcender System as a Senior Fellow at the Wharton School of Business and at other top academic institutions, including the Stanford Graduate School of Business, Northwestern's Kellogg School of Management, and Columbia

Business School. Many of the business executives, professionals, and students in my workshops, seminars, and speaking engagements have described how the Transcender System significantly *transforms* how they think about and compete in business. After participating in one of my firm's seminars, a senior executive told me that the Transcender System is the "world's most powerful winning system for companies and their products."

In *Brands Don't Win*, I am sharing with you the secrets of the three-step Transcender System™. This system is cross-product, cross-geographic, and cross-functional. I will demonstrate how this system works through 16 case studies, showcasing leading "Transcenders" like Apple, Amazon, Starbucks, Nike, Uber, Google, and Peloton. I will highlight successful, diverse products ranging from Glossier Milky Jelly Face Wash and Lemi Shine dishwashing detergent to GEICO car insurance and Tesla electric cars. I have applied this system around the world, from the United States to Europe, Russia to South Africa, Japan to Australia, and most major countries in between.

Importantly, the Transcender System is <u>not</u> a marketing department approach; it is a *company-wide* approach. Companies today no longer win by focusing on marketing and sales; they win with a Campaign Agenda that requires every single employee to believe in, communicate, and champion that Agenda. Companies win when all professionals align with the Campaign Agenda, in the same way that players in an orchestra perform parts from the same score. Therefore, this book applies to you and each of your professional colleagues, regardless of corporate role or market.

Now, are you ready to learn how the best companies play a game only they can win?

## INTRODUCTION SUMMARY

- President John Kennedy and the US won the Space Race by changing the game to the "Man on the Moon" race. This approach is commonly used by politicians during elections. Politicians call it **"Changing the Agenda."** In political terms, a Campaign Agenda is the core, overarching concept that a candidate wants to convey to constituents—as well as the game the candidate wants to force his rivals to play.
- Leading companies, including Apple, Starbucks, and Peloton, also change the business game with what in the Transcender System are called *Campaign Agendas*. They create their own game, execute their Agenda, and force competitors to play by their rules.
- The Transcender System™ is a powerful, proven, and practical approach that all business professionals can learn and apply to help their company win.
- The Transcender System is <u>not</u> a marketing department approach; it is a *company-wide* approach. This system is cross-product, cross-geographic, and cross-functional.

# CHAPTER 1

# The Transcender
# Revolution

Branding has existed for over 4,000 years, beginning with the branding of livestock in the Indus Valley, modern-day India. The term "branding" derives from the Old Norse word *brandr* or "to burn" because early humans would use burned wood to stamp their ownership on livestock. Over centuries, other civilizations increasingly used branding to identify goods, including pottery ("engravings"), bricks ("quarry marks"), paper ("water marks"), and paintings (artists' signatures).

Beginning around 800 BCE in ancient Greece, small entrepreneurs called metics sought to distinguish their pottery and other goods by using early-stage branding tactics. Some international companies have brands dating back over 1,000 years, such as Staffelter Hof Wines (1,156 years) and Chateau de Goulaine Wines (1,018 years). With the Industrial Revolution, branding took off as companies began to move their goods across great distances. To compete with locally recognized and produced goods, these companies used mass-market branding to distinguish their products on the basis of various attributes.

America's oldest brands date back hundreds of years and include both branded products and services; Crane and Co. (paper, in 1799), J.P. Morgan Chase (banking, in 1799), and DuPont (chemicals and science-based products, in 1802) are just three examples. Consumer product companies have continued to evolve, marketing some of the oldest and best-known brands today: Coca-Cola, Heinz Ketchup, Kellogg's cereals, and many others.

Even to this day, **most companies play the exact same game: brand differentiation**. They create a product brand and differentiate the brand by leveraging advertising, promotions, sales representatives, and other tactics. I call these companies "**Traditionalists**" because they all use the conventional model of business competition based on *product selection*: consumers select brands.

However, after nearly four decades of competition consulting and analyzing hundreds of companies and thousands of products, I identified a small but growing group of successful companies that do not play the Traditionalist brand game; they play their own game. I call these companies "**Transcenders**" because they change the game and rise above competitors by using an approach based on *product election*: consumers *elect* products.

These two competitive models represent very distinct systems for product commercialization. The first, which I call the Traditionalist System, is based on a *product playbook*. This system represents the older, more conventional model of competition. Most companies are still operating in this Traditionalist way. The second model, the "Transcender System," is based on a *political playbook*.

## THE RISE OF THE TRANSCENDERS

Why are successful companies increasingly using a political playbook instead of a product playbook? In a word, the Internet. While there were a few Transcender companies prior to the rise of the Internet—notably Nike and Starbucks—most of the companies I'm referring to either originated following the advent of the Internet as dot-coms, or were existing companies, such as Apple, that adopted the Transcender approach.

The Internet has fundamentally changed how companies compete in three very important ways.

First, the availability of the Internet has led to a dramatic increase in the number of competing products. In some cases, brand companies are vying against hundreds or thousands of similar products from other companies all over the world.

Second, due to the availability of the Internet as a marketing channel, the amount of market information and brand advertising has skyrocketed. According to *Forbes*, the average consumer is besieged by as many as 10,000 ads *every day*. Potential customers are overwhelmed by all the product choices, promotional messages, and market noise.

Third, the Internet has also enabled an outpouring of comparative product reviews and data. Potential customers now have real-time, real-world product feedback from user reviews on Amazon and numerous other sites. Today, consumers increasingly perceive actual user feedback as more authentic and reliable than promotional information from brand-biased companies. As a result, there's a growing preference for products with higher user ratings over rival brands with lower ratings, even if those have been the target of higher promotional spending by better-known brand companies. Amazon features many best-selling products with over 15,000 reviews; the Instant Pot Duo 7-in-1 electric pressure cooker, which has 150,000 reviews, and the HSI Professional Glider flat iron hair straightener, with 65,000 reviews, are two examples. Both are produced by relatively small, heretofore unknown brand companies.

In short, product perceptions are increasingly being framed more by customers than by companies. This is the "democratization" of products: products are increasingly being elected, not selected. You will read later about how the fast casual restaurant chain Sweetgreen has democratized "healthy food," and the cosmetics company Glossier has democratized "beauty products." This power shift is undermining the Traditionalist brand game and leveling the playing field for upstarts like Halo Top ice cream and Lemi Shine dishwashing detergent as they compete against brand behemoths Unilever, Procter & Gamble, and others.

In effect, the product competitive landscape increasingly resembles recent US presidential elections. The 2016 Republican presidential primaries started with a field of 17 candidates, the highest number since 1948. At the start of the 2020 Democratic presidential primary campaign, there were 29 candidates—the largest field ever, and far too numerous even to fit all together on stage for a debate.

Voters were overwhelmed by all the politicians, policies, politicking, and messaging. The savviest politicians realized they had to rise above the political fray to stand out—and to transcend their competitors by "owning the narrative."

The way to accomplish that was with a single, overarching, and memorable Campaign Agenda. Obama successfully used this approach in 2008 with his "Change" Agenda. Donald Trump likewise won in 2016 with his simple but effective Campaign Agenda of "Make America Great Again." In 2020, Joe Biden won the "Battle for the Soul of America" by framing the election as a referendum on the character of his rival Donald Trump. Transcender companies usually win against Traditionalist companies in part because of their concise and inspiring political-style communications.

Additionally, Transcender companies gravitate to political playbooks because of the way they inspire followers. People do not vote for political candidates or policies; they vote for beliefs. They want a presidential candidate to improve their lives. In short, voters seek inspiration, not simply information. Increasingly, customers want the same thing: inspiring companies that they believe will enhance their lives. They are often driven more by principles than by products. These customers feel a need to *believe in* a company's Campaign Agenda before they buy the company's products.

## HOW TRANSCENDERS WIN

There are myriad significant differences between the two competitive models, as shown in the chart below.

# Comparison Chart of Key Differences:
## The *Traditionalist* System vs. the *Transcender* System™

| Key Differences | Traditionalist System (Product *Selection*) | Transcender System (Product *Election*) |
|---|---|---|
| *Key to Winning* | Differentiate the Brand | Change the Agenda |
| *Playbook* | Product Playbook | Political Playbook |
| *Product Development* | Evolutionary (Incremental Changes) | Revolutionary (Transcendent Changes) |
| *Campaign Style* | Military Campaign | Election Campaign |
| *Communications* | Brand Messaging (Multiple Different Messages) | Campaign Platform (One Overarching Platform) |
| *Target Audiences* | Customers | Customers and Stakeholders |
| *Marketing Execution* | Marketing Mix ("4 P's") | Winning Actions ("4 A's") |
| *Behavior Change* | Buy In | Believe In |
| *Corporate Objective* | Product Purchase | Transcendent Experience |

Traditionalist companies focus on communicating and promoting the key competitive advantages of their product over a few rival products. They utilize brand or "product differentiation" to convince customers to choose their brand over competitors' brands based on selected features (e.g., faster, longer, stronger) or other benefits. In fact, many Traditionalist companies specifically use competitive products as benchmarks and conduct extensive market research with potential customers to identify better or improved product features and benefits.

Traditionalist marketers ask customers what they want or need. They conduct surveys, focus groups, design meetings, and other types of market research to identify ways to improve on their existing product over competitors' products. They react to customers' feedback. As Apple's former CEO Steve Jobs once said, "You can't just ask customers what they want and then try to give that to them. By the time you get it built, they will want something new." Unfortunately, conventional product development often leads to evolutionary, rather than revolutionary, changes.

For example, Traditionalist rivals Berkshire Hathaway and Eveready Battery Company compete to sell their respective brands Duracell and Energizer in the consumer electronics market. Over time, they have gradually enhanced the performance of and differentiated their brands on the basis of battery life and power, as well as other features.

This conventional approach is in stark contrast to that of Transcenders, who seek to create *revolutionary, game-changing* products. Transcender marketers tell customers what they want. They use their market intuition and out-of-the-box thinking to reimagine products that customers do not even know they want. They "proact," not react. Apple's iPhone, Tesla's electric vehicles, and Google's search engine are perfect examples of transcendent products.

Traditionalist companies typically commercialize their products using a **military-style campaign.** Their goal is twofold: 1) to win by differentiating their product brand, based on superior features and benefits; and 2) to overwhelm competitors with significantly greater investments and better promotional tactics. Traditionalists usually prepare to launch products, almost like an army invasion, into their target sector or customer segment. After developing secret military-type strategic plans, they initiate their market assault with extensive, heavy "air cover" in the form of advertising and promotions. In some cases, this assault is followed by the launch of a "ground attack" led by legions of sales or account representatives. These brand battles wage on for years, as rivals fight for their market turf.

In contrast, Transcender companies win by Changing the Agenda, forcing competitors to play their game. Transcenders conduct **election-style campaigns** to commercialize their products, which are often specifically designed to be disruptive or unconventional. Like US presidential campaigns, these companies take three steps: 1) Create the Agenda, 2) Communicate the Agenda, and 3) Champion the Agenda. They communicate their Campaign Platform to push their Campaign Agenda and position their product "candidate" with influential "stakeholders."

Such stakeholders might include product pundits or experts, financial and market analysts, journalists and other media representatives, big-name partners and purchasers, consumer influencers or bloggers, and others. These powerful constituencies are analogous to the 538 Electoral College delegates in US elections. Presidential candidates know that they must win the Electoral College vote—not the popular vote—to become president. Similarly, Transcender companies recognize they must win with their stakeholders, because they are so influential on customers and other purchasers. Politicians realize they must own the narrative and the airwaves to win a presidential election. Transcender companies also leverage the media and media influencers—stakeholders—to win product elections.

Notably, **Transcenders *lead* with the Campaign Agenda and *follow* with the brand.** They use branding to support their Campaign Agenda, but they do <u>not</u> win by focusing on their brands. Instead, Transcenders create and communicate a single-page, overarching Campaign Platform that is repeatedly blasted out to the entire stakeholder ecosystem. These companies conduct these election-style campaigns to own the online and offline media airwaves with consistent, concise communications.

For more than 60 years, Traditionalist companies have deployed the conventional marketing toolbox, made up of the "4 P's": Product (good or service), Price (cost of the product), Place (distribution channels), and Promotion. There is a heavy emphasis on tactics such as advertising, promotions, sales forces, and account representatives. Traditionalists typically leverage overwhelming promotions to help win brand battles.

Transcender companies do not rely on such rudimentary promotional tactics to win. They leverage more sophisticated winning Actions, which are based on what I call the "4 A's": *Access, Advantages, Advangelicals,* and *Awareness.* These Actions are cross-functional, cross-disciplinary, and cross-geographic activities designed to push the company's Campaign Agenda. I will discuss these Actions in detail later in the book.

Traditionalists want customers to "buy into" their sales pitches and purchase their products. In contrast, Transcenders go beyond product purchases to offer a *transcendent product experience*; they want their customers and other stakeholders to "believe in" and share their product experience with others. The Transcender System enables companies and business professionals to rise above all the Traditionalist companies by playing at a totally different level.

## A REVOLUTIONARY WAY TO WIN

After nearly 4,000 years of branding, the increasing conversion of leading companies to the Transcender approach represents a true paradigm shift in how businesses operate. Dr. Andrew Finn, Associate Professor of Communication at George Mason University, explains that "a paradigm shift occurs when there is a crisis in a particular field… The old paradigm can no longer account for enough of the existing evidence. Eventually, the old view is replaced by the new view because it is a closer approximation of reality." That is, the framework fits better with the available evidence, creating a new view of the world. Paradigm shifts are *revolutionary*, not evolutionary.

A classic example of a paradigm shift was the revelation that the Earth was round, not flat. In the 5th century BC, the Greek philosopher Pythagoras was the first to suggest that the Earth was spherical, but this fact was not proven until the Portuguese explorer Ferdinand Magellan and his crew circumnavigated the globe in 1519–1522.

Paradigm shifts shape how we interpret facts, and how we see, think, feel, and behave. The paradigm shift of the Transcender System—*from product selection to product election*—has revolutionized how companies compete. The Transcender approach runs counter to four millennia of branding and centuries of winning with brand differentiation. How companies adapt to this Transcender shift will increasingly determine if they win.

Companies that quickly grasp the magnitude of this shift and effectively leverage the Transcender System experience dramatically better product launches, sales, profits, and impact.

Importantly, Transcenders do not win by differentiating their brand; they win by *Changing the Agenda*. These companies are revolutionizing the business world by forcing rivals to play their game. In the next chapter, I will explain how we can look to US presidential campaigns to understand how to Change the Agenda.

## CHAPTER 1 SUMMARY

- Branding has existed for over 4,000 years, beginning with the branding of livestock in the Indus Valley. The Industrial Revolution spurred the development of mass-market consumer brand companies. **Currently, most companies play the same game: brand differentiation.** They create a product brand and differentiate that brand by leveraging advertising, promotions, sales representatives, and other tactics. I call these companies "**Traditionalists**" because they all use a conventional product playbook.
- **However, primarily because of the internet, there are a small but growing number of successful companies that do not play the Traditionalist brand game; they play their own game.** I call these companies "**Transcenders**" because they change the game and rise above competitors by using a **political playbook** to win.
  - Transcender companies do not win by differentiating their brand; they win by **Changing the Agenda**.
  - Transcender companies conduct **election campaigns—not military campaigns**—to commercialize their products.

- The Traditionalist System and the Transcender System represent two very different competitive models for product commercialization. The Internet has dramatically increased the number of companies using the Transcender System.
- The conventional worldview of the Traditionalist System is increasingly being challenged by an entirely new Transcender worldview. This paradigm shift—**from product selection to product election**—has fundamentally transformed how companies compete.
- Companies and professionals who grasp this revolutionary shift and approach product commercialization like elections are demonstrating dramatically better product sales.

# CHAPTER 2

# Winning with a Political Playbook

*Products today are elected, not selected.* If you want your product to win, just study US presidential elections. Certain presidential campaigns provide a powerful blueprint that can help companies and professionals succeed. I could have chosen several different winning presidential candidates as examples, but I've selected Barack Obama's first election campaign in 2008 because it clearly models the three fundamental steps in the Transcender System: *Create, Communicate,* and *Champion* the Campaign Agenda.

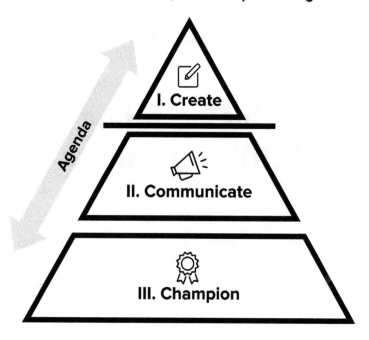

## The Transcender System™:
### Create, Communicate, and Champion the *Agenda*

Agenda

I. Create

II. Communicate

III. Champion

**CASE STUDY: HOW OBAMA WON BY CHANGING THE GAME***

When Senator Barack Obama took the stage at the Democratic National Convention (DNC) in Boston in 2004, the headline in the *Philadelphia Inquirer* read, "Who the Heck Is This Guy?" Most US voters had never heard of him. Even fewer knew at the time that he was unofficially launching his 2008 presidential campaign more than *four years* prior to that election. However, Obama and his confidants were aware that several former presidents—including Franklin D. Roosevelt

---

\* *The presentation of politician/political case studies does not in any way reflect my support for or against any politician, party, or campaign. I use these political examples strictly to help readers better understand the Transcender System.*

and Bill Clinton—had launched their presidential campaigns with rousing presidential nomination speeches on the big stage at previous DNCs.

At the beginning of his speech, Obama alluded to the fact that he personally represented change by virtue of his race and background. He acknowledged how his "presence on this stage is pretty unlikely"; that his father was a foreign student raised in Kenya, and his grandfather a domestic British servant; that his parents gave him "an African name, Barack, or 'blessed,' believing that in a tolerant America your name is no barrier to success"; and that he was "grateful for the diversity of my heritage."

He continued to discuss how more change was needed in America: "And fellow Americans—Democrats, Republicans, Independents—I say to you tonight: we have more work to do… People do not expect government to solve all their problems. But they sense, deep in their bones, that with just a slight change in priorities, we can make sure that every child in America has a decent shot at life, and that the doors of opportunity remain open to all. They know we can do better. And they want that choice."

## STEP #1: CREATE THE AGENDA

Obama first introduced his Campaign Agenda of Change during his DNC speech in 2004. Over the next four years, Obama consistently pushed this Agenda in numerous public statements:

*"Change will not come if we wait for some other person or some other time. We are the ones we've been waiting for. We are the change that we seek."*

*"Never stop believing in the power of your ideas, your imagination, your hard work to change the world."*

*"Change is never easy, but always possible."*

*"Change doesn't come from Washington. Change comes to Washington."*

*"Your voice can change the world."*

The Obama campaign employed a variety of slogans, including "Change and Hope"; "Yes, We Can"; and "Change We Can Believe In." He and his advisors ultimately settled on a single word for his Campaign Agenda: Change.

In election terms, a Campaign Agenda is the core, overarching concept that a candidate conveys to voters, and the game the candidate forces his rivals to play. For instance, a US presidential candidate who is very experienced in foreign policy may want to focus voters on foreign policy, while his rival may want to focus on domestic policy. Whichever candidate can influence the electorate to buy into and support his/her Campaign Agenda usually wins the election.

Obama wanted voters to view the 2008 presidential election as a referendum on change and see the contest through his lens of the need for change in America. He was framing the election on his terms: if voters and other constituents looked through his lens and bought into the need for change, then he represented the only true "Change Candidate," in contrast to "more of the same" McCain. Obama was effectively forcing his rivals and voters to play a game only he could win.

When Obama officially announced his presidential campaign on February 10, 2007, in Springfield, Illinois, he said, "I recognize there is a certain presumptuousness in this—a certain audacity—to this announcement," he said. "I know that I haven't spent a lot of time learning the ways of Washington. But I've been there long enough to know that the ways of Washington must change." On the evening of the first Democratic Primary in the 2008 presidential election in New Hampshire, Obama said, "We know the battle ahead will be long, but always remember that no matter what obstacles stand in our way, nothing can withstand the power of millions of voices calling for change." Obama incorporated the word "change" into nearly every speech, interview, press release, and debate, including 11 times during the three debates with the Republican presidential nominee, Senator John McCain.

In stark contrast, the McCain campaign switched from message to message and never adopted a single, overarching Campaign Agenda. For example, on the day that the bankruptcy of the investment firm Lehman Brothers created a financial crisis, McCain proclaimed that the economy was "strong." A few hours later, the *New York Times* reported that "he was backpedaling, and he was calling the economic situation 'a total crisis' and denouncing 'greed' on Wall Street and in Washington." Similarly, McCain initially warned against excessive government intervention in the mortgage crisis, but a month later he changed his position and released a government plan to help people retain their homes. Further demonstrating his campaign's lack of consistency, McCain—during his prime-time speech for the Republican nomination—even tried to steal Obama's Campaign Agenda of change: "Let me offer an advance warning to the old, big-spending, do-nothing, me-first, country-second Washington crowd: change is coming," he said.

Throughout his campaign, Obama consistently advocated for change in nearly every major policy arena, including tax cuts for working families; reducing US dependence on Mideast oil; "affordable, accessible health care" for all Americans; and an end to the Iraq War. Importantly, Obama's Campaign Agenda could be interpreted by voters in whatever way they personally desired. This was part of the success of the Obama Campaign Agenda: it substantiated potential interpretations of what "Change" could mean but did not limit voters to those interpretations.

## STEP #2: COMMUNICATE THE AGENDA

Political candidates use a Campaign Platform to communicate and push their Campaign Agenda. For the Transcender System, I created and use a *modified* version of a political Campaign Platform that incorporates the Campaign Agenda and other key communications into a single, succinct page. Below is my summary of Senator Obama's 2008 Campaign Platform, using Transcender System terms:

## Senator Obama's 2008 Presidential Campaign Platform

| | |
|---|---|
| ***CAMPAIGN AGENDA***<br>*The "game" the candidate*<br>*wants to play (≤5 words)* | **CHANGE** |
| ***CAMPAIGN C-MESSAGES***<br>*Concise communications to*<br>*push the Agenda (3 max)* | • "Change We Can Believe In"<br>• "Yes, We Can"<br>• "Change and Hope" |
| ***CAMPAIGN CANDIDATE***<br>*Candidate that best fulfills*<br>*the Campaign Agenda or*<br>*plays that game* | **Senator Obama** |
| ***CANDIDATE POSITIONING***<br>*Perception to be created for*<br>*the Candidate in the minds*<br>*of stakeholders (≤5 words)* | **The Change Candidate** |
| ***P-BITES***<br>*Concise Candidate Messages*<br>*that describe the Candidate*<br>*(3 max, each ≤5 words)* | • Hopeful<br>• Progressive<br>• Audacious |
| ***COMPETITOR***<br>***COUNTER-POSITIONING***<br>*Perception to be created for*<br>*rivals in the minds of key*<br>*stakeholders (<5 words)* | *Hillary Clinton and John*<br>*McCain: "Same Old*<br>*Washington Politicians"* |

The Transcender System Campaign Platform consists of six key components: *Campaign Agenda, C-Messages, Candidate, Positioning, P-Bites,* and *Counter-Positioning.*

**Campaign Agenda:** While most politicians use as many as five words, Obama's campaign demonstrated the power of owning a single word: "Change." Notice that his campaign did not lead with the name of the candidate Obama as its brand. Obama's team knew that it had to get voters to believe in the *need for change* before they would accept the first African American Democratic nominee, much less one championing many potential policy changes.

**C-Messages:** The team supported the Campaign Agenda with a few, concise Campaign Messages (C-Messages). C-Messages are designed to help push and communicate the Campaign Agenda, not the candidate or product. Typically, they use short phrases to repeat the key word(s) from the Campaign Agenda. Obama's C-Messages were "Change We Can Believe In," "Yes, We Can," and "Change and Hope."

**Candidate:** Importantly, the team recognized that it was far more important to push the Campaign Agenda, Change, *before* the Candidate (Brand), Obama. This is an important lesson for professionals using the Transcender System: **Lead with the Agenda; follow with the Brand.** Just remember, "A before B." Elected politicians and Transcender companies win by promoting their Agenda rather than promoting their brand, the older approach used by Traditionalist companies.

**Positioning:** Positioning is the perception that a politician or company wants to create in the minds of its target audiences. Positioning in the Transcender System differs from the Traditionalist concept of brand positioning in three ways.

First, as mentioned above, the brand positioning *follows* the Campaign Agenda; Transcenders focus on showcasing their Agenda, not their brand.

Second, I use the term "Positioning" instead of the common

advertising term, "product positioning statements." Many Traditionalist companies use long product positioning statements, while Transcender companies use five words or fewer to position their product or services.

Third, unlike Traditionalist brand positioning, Transcender System Positioning employs the same term or term(s) as those in the Agenda. Ideally, it is the candidate or product that best fulfills the proposed Campaign Agenda or best plays that game. For example, Obama's team positioned him as "the candidate for change," which directly aligned with the overarching agenda of Change. I refer to this as Agenda-Positioning Alignment or Double Alignment: the Positioning of the candidate or product echoes the same wording as the Agenda. If voters recognized the need for change, Obama represented the only presidential candidate capable of accomplishing this change. Likewise, Transcender companies position their products in stakeholders' minds with one or a few key words that align with their overall Campaign Agenda.

**P-Bites:** P-Bites normally mean Product Bites—concise product messages—but here I will use the term to mean "Presidential Bites." Instead of numerous lengthy messages about the candidate, the Obama team described him with three short and simple P-Bites: "Hopeful," "Progressive," and "Audacious." In fact, Obama titled his pre-election 2006 book *The Audacity of Hope: Thoughts on Reclaiming the American Dream*. Similarly, instead of numerous brand messages, Transcender companies use two or three "P-Bites," each typically five words or fewer, to describe their products. In the Transcender System, P-Bites effectively *replace* longer brand messages to be more memorable.

**Counter-Positioning:** Obama rarely mentioned his rivals,

Democratic challenger Senator Hillary Clinton and Republican nominee Senator John McCain, by name—an *indirect* Counter-Positioning technique. When he did refer to them, he created the perception that they were the "same old Washington politicians"—a stark contrast to his positioning as the "Change Candidate."

In contrast, Republican nominee Donald Trump used *direct* counter-positioning in his successful 2016 presidential bid. For example, he counter positioned his chief rival Hillary Clinton by repeatedly calling her "Crooked Hillary." He effectively changed her name from "Hillary Clinton" to "Crooked Hillary." While this is considered a very extreme political approach, I mention it to highlight the potential power of both *direct* and *indirect* counter-positioning. As with presidential candidates, Transcender companies can also effectively counter position their competitors and their products, using either indirect or direct approaches.

## STEP #3: CHAMPION THE AGENDA

Obama's team consistently repeated the same Campaign Agenda to potential voters. *The New Republic*'s Thomas B. Edsall stated that "the Obama operation's outreach was expert, prolonged, and coherent. Over the duration of the campaign, Obama's forces sent out over one billion emails and communicated by text messaging with over one million voters."

However, to win a presidential or product election, it is not enough to Create the Agenda and Communicate the Agenda. You must *Champion the Agenda* to force competitors to play your game. Obama leveraged what I call the "winning Actions" to Champion the Agenda. Winning Actions are cross-functional, cross-disciplinary, and cross-geographic activities designed to push the Campaign Agenda. There are four types of winning Actions:

1. *Access*: Making products available to customers in ways that are either limited (e.g., Zara's limited apparel promotions) or unlimited (e.g., Google's access to information).
2. *Advantages*: Offering transcendent product features, either intrinsic to it (e.g., Tesla cars) or extending beyond the product itself (e.g., buying Tesla cars will move along "The Transition to Sustainable Energy").
3. *Advangelicals*: Deploying political or corporate campaign supporters who advocate and evangelize the Campaign Agenda to other constituents or customers.
4. *Awareness*: Creating significant buzz or excitement for the Campaign Agenda.

The ultimate objective of these winning Actions is to push the Campaign Agenda with customers and stakeholders so that they believe in and support the Agenda, ultimately purchasing a company's products or, in the case of elections, voting for the candidate. Here are some of the ways that Obama implemented winning Actions to push his Campaign Agenda of change.

### Obama Winning Action #1: Accessing Private Funding and Early Voting

Obama changed the game in campaign fundraising. He became the first major presidential party nominee in history to refuse public funds for the general election. Instead, Obama accessed private donor funding, primarily through the Internet, from activists, millennials, minority groups, and other individuals. This novel grassroots approach raised nearly $750 million, breaking previous presidential primary and general election campaign records.

Obama also capitalized on early voting in states that permitted it. He and his campaign team had anticipated that Internet-empowered voters, with ready access to all types of information, would make much earlier decisions about presidential candidates than voters had in previous campaigns. According to media consultant Pete Snyder, the Obama team believed that the traditional timetable for voters to select their candidate had fundamentally shifted from the traditional 72 hours before Election Day to weeks, or even months, prior to the election.

Implementing this unconventional strategy, Obama conducted his most intensive campaigning early in the cycle. By outspending McCain by almost 10 to 1 during the usually slow summer months preceding the election, Obama was, for example, able to capture Virginia, a traditionally Republican state, which permitted its citizens to start casting their ballots six weeks before the day of the election. In the final analysis, the Obama team had been correct: over one-third of all 2008 presidential votes were cast prior to Election Day, twice the proportion of early votes cast in the 2000 election.

By starting his campaign early and aggressively, Obama shaped voter opinions ahead of his opponent, drove fundraising money and volunteers into his campaign, and ultimately won the election. Obama's national field director, Jon Carson, said that **"early voting didn't change our strategy. It was our strategy."**

*Obama Winning Action #2: Leveraging Technology to Gain Competitive Advantage*

The Obama campaign team employed cutting-edge technology to gain a competitive advantage. In a 2008 *Wired* article, journalist Sarah Lai Stirland detailed how the Obama team developed a social media network site, my.BarackObama.com, as the foundation for their organizational infrastructure. Nicknamed "MyBO," this site equipped local Obama volunteers with a Neighbor-to-Neighbor tool to identify local registered voters so that they could convince them to vote for Obama. For example, in the critical swing state of Florida, the Obama team used the website to deploy 230,000 volunteers, divided into 19,000 neighborhood teams and directed by 500 paid campaign field organizers, to target potential Obama voters in 1,400 focus neighborhoods. Stirland explained: "The Obama campaign has the most sophisticated organizing apparatus of any presidential campaign in history…erecting a vast, intricate machine set to fuel an unprecedented get-out-the-vote drive."

This integration of technology and advocacy gave Obama a tremendous competitive advantage over his rival McCain, whose campaign suffered from limited technology-enabled capabilities. Obama effectively leveraged the Internet to rally supporters, showcase his policies, and procure funding. McCain was unable to overcome Obama's transcendent advantage in technology.

*Obama Winning Action #3: Creating an "Advangelical" Movement*

Importantly, Obama was not only conducting a presidential campaign; he was creating a movement. The best presidential campaigns—and product campaigns—create an overwhelming movement of "Advangelicals," a portmanteau I coined to describe political and corporate campaign supporters who advocate and evangelize the Campaign Agenda. These winning campaigns ignite passion, inspire people, and rally zealots for a cause that they can believe in. David Gergen said that, "Obama has been a pioneer in joining the powers of the Internet with the principles of community organizing. Howard Dean used the Internet for meetups—Obama used it to *create a movement*."

Obama rallied new and different types of voters to his Campaign Agenda of Change: young voters, small donors, minorities, ethnic groups, and others who believed it was time for a change. And he regularly communicated his Campaign Agenda and Platform to all his constituents. As the most technologically savvy presidential candidate in history, Obama used social media sites such as Myspace and Facebook to update, engage, and galvanize supporters, who then formed their own nationwide online communities to support his Campaign Agenda.

This approach worked especially well for voters under the age of 30, nearly two-thirds of whom voted for Obama. The divergence between younger and older voters in 2008 was the highest since exit polling began in 1972. More diverse racially and ethnically, these younger voters supported many and sometimes all of Obama's campaign policies, including a more activist government, opposition to the war in Iraq, and less social conservatism. According to a *CNBC.com* report following the election, "[The youth vote] is turning states that [Obama] would've lost or barely won into more comfortable margins," said John Della Volpe, the director of polling for the Harvard University Institute of Politics. "Not only are they voting in higher numbers, but they are also voting more Democratic."

Peter D. Hart, a polling expert for *NBC News* and *The Wall Street*

*Journal*, said in 2008, "This was an election of firsts. It is the first modern election where technology enabled supporters to play a direct role in the campaign. It is the first election where citizen media dominated the dialogue... It was a total transformation. The rules have been rewritten, and we're never going to go back and play politics in the same way." In 2008, Obama's use of technology to attract, inspire, and organize Advangelicals permanently changed the political game of winning presidential elections.

### Obama Winning Action #4: Creating Awareness with the CHANGE Poster

Artist Shepard Fairey designed the so-called "HOPE Poster," a stylized red, beige, and blue image of Obama. He originally titled the poster "PROGRESS," but soon substituted the word "HOPE," and finally, "CHANGE." The design became a pop culture phenomenon and an iconic symbol of Obama's Campaign Agenda. Fairey initially produced only 350 of the posters, but demand escalated quickly; Obama's Advangelicals were highly motivated to spread the image far and wide. As Fairey recalls, *"We sent posters to Philadelphia and they got put up all over—on abandoned buildings and on street corners. That is something you don't normally see—that level of motivation in people to spread an image."* The CHANGE posters visually and verbally created enormous awareness for Obama's Campaign Agenda of Change, which he first communicated four years earlier.

The reaction to Obama's stirring 2004 Democratic National Convention speech had been overwhelmingly positive. In the *Beacon Broadside,* Mary Frances Berry and Josh Gottheimer reported, "The reviews were unanimous: it was a barnburner. People immediately compared his oratorical skills to those of

John Kennedy, Ronald Reagan, and Martin Luther King Jr. He was mobbed by crowds, not just that evening, but also every day thereafter... His political future would be forever changed." The authors quoted Senator Dick Durbin of Illinois: "Without that Boston speech, there is a question whether Barack would be...[president] today. His public image changed because of that speech."

Obama's electrifying 2004 DNC address catapulted him onto the national stage and into instantaneous presidential contention. Four years later, he achieved a surprise victory in the Iowa Democratic caucus, the first delegate-choosing event of the presidential campaign season, establishing himself as a credible contender for the US presidency.

On November 4, 2008, Obama was declared the winner of the 2008 presidential election. During his victory speech that night in Grant Park in Chicago, he reiterated his Campaign Agenda: "This victory alone is not the change we seek—it is only the chance for us to make that change." Obama also acknowledged that night, "It's been a long time coming, but tonight, because of what we did on this day, in this election, at this defining moment, change has come to America." In a 2008 *Huffington Post* article, contributor Kerry Candaele noted that in that speech, the opening words of his statement had been adapted from gospel and R&B singer Sam Cooke's 1964 single "Change is Gonna Come," which had been adopted as a 1960's civil rights anthem.

In becoming America's first African American president, Obama had effectively come full circle from his 2004 DNC speech, in which he had called out how his African heritage represented a dramatic—indeed, unique—change among presidential candidates. The headline in the *Philadelphia Inquirer* on the morning following the election declared that it was a "historic win," and repeated his words from the night before: "President-Elect Obama: *Change Has Come to America.*"

In a 2008 interview with *Rolling Stone*, longtime former senior presidential advisor David Gergen summarized how Obama won: "The key, in my judgment, was that early on, Obama forged a strategy for victory, assembled a team around that strategy, and executed the best-organized and most brilliant campaign we've seen in American politics since John Kennedy in 1960."

## OBAMA'S THREE-STEP POLITICAL PLAYBOOK

Obama's successful strategy centered on his three-step political playbook. The most successful companies follow the same three Transcender System steps. They **create** a memorable Campaign Agenda, typically five words or fewer. They consistently and repeatedly **communicate** their Campaign Agenda and Platform to their targeted potential customers and other stakeholders. And they **champion** the Campaign Agenda with a few prioritized, powerful winning Actions.

## CHAPTER 2 SUMMARY

- US presidential election campaigns provide a clear blueprint for helping products, companies, and professionals become winners. The **Transcender System™** for businesses is modeled on US presidential elections and consists of three major steps: *Create the Agenda*, *Communicate the Agenda*, and *Champion the Agenda*.

- Senator Barack Obama's 2008 presidential election campaign expertly exhibits these three fundamental steps for winning presidential campaigns. Obama led with his one-word Campaign Agenda of Change and followed with his Positioning as the "Change Candidate." These are core elements of the Transcender System for companies: **Lead with the Agenda ("A") and follow with the Brand ("B")**.

- Political candidates communicate using a one-page **Campaign Platform** to push their Campaign Agenda. A Campaign Platform incorporates six key communication components: *Campaign Agenda, C-Messages, Candidate, Positioning, P-Bites*, and *Counter-Positioning*.

- To Champion the Agenda, politicians and business professionals leverage the four types of winning **Actions**: *Access, Advantages, Advangelicals*, and *Awareness*.

# CREATE THE AGENDA

# CHAPTER 3

## Play Your Game

Changing the Campaign Agenda means forcing competitors to play your game. What do I mean by "play your game"? When a company creates a situation where they can set their own rules, they impel competitors to react, and ultimately gain significant competitive advantage in their market. Companies that play their game usually win the game because they created it.

I will illustrate the play your game principle with three different examples from the military, sports, and politics.

### MILITARY EXAMPLE: DAVID VS. GOLIATH

More than 3,000 years ago, the Israelite army led by King Saul confronted Philistine invaders on the opposite side of the Elah Valley. Instead of attacking the Israelites from the depth of the valley, the Philistines challenged the Israelites to offer a single combatant to fight against their mammoth warrior, Goliath of Gath. When the Israelite King Saul asked for volunteers to confront the giant Goliath, not a single soldier in his army volunteered. Why would anyone be crazy enough to fight a massive, 6' 9", trained infantry professional, armed with a javelin, spear, and sword, and protected by full body armor? Despite these daunting risks, a shepherd boy named David volunteered.

King Saul initially was reluctant to allow such a small, inexperienced boy to fight the colossus. But David was confident. He was not going to play Goliath's game. Everyone except David assumed that the battle would be "close combat": two men fighting in close quarters with standard sword and spear weaponry. David knew he had to change the fight to win. He was not going anywhere near Goliath; instead, he was going to play his own game of "aerial combat."

David had developed expertise with a sling, a projectile weapon designed to hurl rocks to protect his flock of sheep. Normally, David would have to hit moving targets, such as lions or other wild animals attempting to prey on his sheep. Goliath, on the other hand, was a huge, immobile target with poor eyesight, unable to dodge a small, dense stone speeding toward him with the impact nearing that of a 45-caliber bullet. Unarmored and unafraid, David ran at Goliath and released his stone projectile, hitting him directly in the forehead and killing him.

Here is my analysis of the two different games that David and Goliath were seeking to play:

# Goliath vs. David: Two Different Games

| Characteristics | Goliath | David |
|---|---|---|
| Game | Close Combat | Aerial Combat |
| Physical Attributes | Giant, Military Man | Small, Shepherd Boy |
| Military Approach | Infantry | Slinger |
| Weapons | • Javelin, Spear, Sword<br>• Full Body Armor | • Sling<br>• Rocks |
| Strengths | • Huge Size<br>• Strength | • Slinging<br>• Creativity |
| Weaknesses | • Immobile<br>• Poor Vision | • Small Size<br>• Weak |

Clearly, David forced Goliath to play his aerial combat game and won. This is an important lesson: **Transcenders do not necessarily need to have the most resources, largest marketing budget, or biggest sales force to win.** In fact, Transcenders often spend dramatically less on brand advertising and promotions than Traditionalist companies. This is one of the reasons why smaller—including startup and entrepreneurial—companies have a dramatically better fighting chance, and represent a greater threat, against larger companies in the Transcender world. The Transcender System significantly levels the playing field for all competitors.

## SPORTS EXAMPLE: MESSI VS. FEDERER

In the Traditionalist System, the key to winning is "brand differentiation": find and communicate distinctions between your brand and rivals' brands. Imagine comparing the two top soccer stars of our generation: Argentina's Lionel Messi and Portugal's Cristiano Ronaldo. The key Traditionalist question is always "*Which brand is differentiated?*" In terms of major soccer awards, Messi currently has won six Golden Balls, six Golden Boots, and one FIFA System Player of the Year Award. Similarly, Ronaldo has won five Golden Balls, four Golden Boots, and two FIFA System Player of the Year Awards. Many consider Messi to be the better playmaker and passer, while Ronaldo is regarded as the better finisher and scorer.

For argument's sake, let us say that Messi is slightly differentiated as the best soccer player in the world. However, if you forced Messi to compete in a totally different sport against a top athlete, he would not stand a chance. For example, if he played tennis against Roger Federer, or any other top-ranked tennis professional, Messi would get destroyed. This is the "play your game" concept. It is no longer about differentiating your brand, but rather forcing competitors to play your game.

Therefore, the key question in the Transcender System is "*What game is being played?*" In the coming chapters, I will share examples and case studies of companies forcing their competitors to play their games.

## POLITICAL EXAMPLE: DONALD TRUMP'S 2016 ELECTION CAMPAIGN VS. HILLARY CLINTON*

The primary reason that Donald Trump won the 2016 presidential election is that he forced his rival Hillary Clinton to play his game. Trump consistently and concisely communicated his four-word Campaign Agenda of "**Make America Great Again**"; in stark contrast, Clinton communicated multiple Campaign Agendas during her campaign.

Ironically, Trump first started using the Campaign Agenda of "Make America Great Again" the day after Obama won his 2012 presidential reelection against Mitt Romney. Trump adopted— and improved upon—two key techniques from Obama's 2008 election playbook. Like Obama's "Change" poster, Trump used a simple but powerful visual image: the ubiquitous Make America Great Again or "MAGA" hats. He regularly wore the red hats with the white MAGA phrase, which became very popular with his followers. At one point, his campaign reportedly spent more on the $25 MAGA hats than on polling, consultants, and television commercials. Trump claimed "millions" of hats had been sold.

Like Obama, Trump extensively used social media, but with a far greater focus on Twitter. In 2017, Trump acknowledged the role social media played in his victory when he tweeted, "I won the 2016 election with interviews, speeches and social media… We will continue to WIN! My use of social media is not Presidential - it's MODERN DAY PRESIDENTIAL. Make America Great Again!"

---

* *The presentation of politician/political case studies does not in any way reflect my support for or against any politician, party, or campaign. I use these political examples strictly to help readers better understand the Transcender System.*

In fact, during the first six months of 2017, Trump tweeted "Make America Great Again" 33 times. During the election, his two most used Twitter hashtags after #trump2016 were #makeamericagreatagain and its acronym #maga. Trump averaged nearly twice as many daily Twitter mentions as Clinton.

Trump's unconventional, Twitter-based campaign generated billions of dollars in free advertising—over $3 billion during the first half of 2016 alone. Trump spent dramatically less per vote and per electoral delegate than any other Republican or Democratic presidential candidate, including less than one-third ($4.62/vote) the cost of what Hillary Clinton spent ($14.55/vote). This is typical of Transcender companies, as well: they seek to generate more "earned," or unpaid, media publicity, while Traditionalists spend more on paid advertising and promotions.

During Trump's 2015-2016 election campaign, I was conducting client workshops in the US, Europe, Asia, and Australia. Everywhere I visited, I asked the question: "What is Donald Trump's Campaign Agenda or slogan?" Virtually *every* workshop participant—US and non-US—would respond with "Make America Great Again." When I next asked, "What is Hillary Clinton's Campaign Agenda or slogan?" I received blank stares—from even the US attendees—or at best, an outdated Clinton slogan.

Unlike Trump's Campaign Agenda, why couldn't anyone remember Clinton's Campaign Agenda? Because she had numerous campaign slogans. I have identified at least *seven*:

## SELECTED CLINTON 2016 PRESIDENTIAL CAMPAIGN SLOGANS

1. "Four Fights for America"

2. "Breaking Down Barriers"
3. "Make America Whole"
4. "Providing Real Results"
5. "I'm With Her"
6. "Fighting for Us"
7. "Stronger Together"

The media recognized that Clinton was not prioritizing and communicating a single Campaign Agenda. Six months before the 2016 election, a *Boston Globe* article headline stated, "Clinton's Message Keeps Evolving." Hillary Clinton had so many slogans that she confused voters. In fact, her own husband, former President Bill Clinton, misstated her final 2016 slogan while campaigning for her in North Carolina just *two weeks* before the presidential election: "This campaign slogan of Hillary's, 'Growing Together,' is more than just two words that sound good," Bill Clinton told the crowd. The real campaign slogan was "Stronger Together."

On September 13, 2016, *The Wall Street Journal* ran an article headline stating: "Hillary Clinton's Larger Dilemma: Playing Donald Trump's Game, Or Not?" In a 2016 interview with *TheJournal.ie*, political advisor Eoghan McDermott pointed out that Clinton spent a lot of time reacting to issues "which again you could say is partly due to Trump's capacity to dictate the agenda, which led her to fighting on his territory."

Ultimately, she was forced to play Trump's game and lost the 2016 presidential election. In the book *Shattered: Inside Hillary Clinton's Doomed Campaign*, co-written by Jonathan Allen and Amie Parnes, two journalists who closely followed her 2016 presidential campaign, the authors assert the primary reason Clinton failed was that she and the campaign team "never found a good way (or at least a way she embraces) that sums up her vision for how America would be different."

**In the Transcender System, if you have more than one Campaign Agenda—like Clinton—then you have none.** In fact, multiple Campaign Agendas *compete* against each other. Effectively, Clinton was competing against multiple presidential candidate versions of herself. Because Clinton had so many Campaign Agendas and messages (her campaign website had nearly 40 pages outlining policy positions versus the seven pages on Trump's website), she was tuned out by many voters, while many voters responded to Trump's singular Campaign Agenda of Make America Great Again.

Dr. Nelson Cowan, Curators' Distinguished Professor of Psychological Sciences at the University of Missouri, who specializes in memory research, said that it is "more important for political campaigns to have a short message." He noted that if a presenter—like Clinton—communicates too much extraneous information at once, people will find that amount of input to be overwhelming and tune out.

A simple analogy makes this clear. If you were to listen to a symphony orchestra, and each musical section were playing a different song—percussionists one song, the winds a different song—you would likely cover your ears and tune out the noise, much like many voters did with Clinton's many Campaign Agendas. In the best presidential and product campaigns, everyone and every message must consistently communicate the exact same Campaign Agenda or "sing" from the same song sheet.

This concept of a single Campaign Agenda has profound implications for products and branding. In the Traditionalist System, companies communicate numerous brand messages, supported by extensive advertising, promotions, and often sales representatives or account managers. More is considered more. But in the Transcender System, *less is considered more*: one overarching Campaign Agenda supported by at most two or three short Campaign Messages ("C-Messages").

Presidential candidate Trump was so successful in communicating and convincing voters of his single, simple Campaign Agenda of "Make America Great Again" because he used the "framing effect." The framing effect is a form of cognitive bias where people select an option based on whether it is presented in a positive (e.g., glass half full) or a negative light (glass half empty), as a loss or as a gain. Frames are essentially the lens through which we see the world.

The framing effect can also be used to change belief systems. For example, if I took you to an Iowa farmhouse and asked you to look out the window frame, you would likely see a flat field and believe the earth is flat (assuming you did not know otherwise). However, if I then took you up to the International Space Station and asked you to look out the station's window frame, you would clearly see that the world is round. The key takeaway is that the specific frame through which you look at the world will dictate what you see, think, and believe.

Creating the Agenda—or the "lens"—is a powerful example of the framing effect in practice. Transcenders ensure their stakeholders view the world through their lens. There are two important observations regarding framing. First, a person cannot hear or see frames. They are part of your unconscious mental state, so that an individual is not aware of its effects.

Second, frames are more effective and lasting the more times they are deployed. This was what made Trump's constant repetition of his Campaign Agenda "Make America Great Again" so influential. Trump wanted voters to see his version of a greater America through his lens.

Dr. Cowan has found that humans remember words they hear more efficiently if they are made to fit into that person's existing belief system. Trump's followers more readily bought into his ideas because Trump had already created the frame of reference or belief system of "Make America Great Again." President Trump's successful 2016 presidential campaign supports ongoing psychological research that demonstrates the power of framing, not only on presidential elections but also on everyday choices, such as product preferences.

Ironically, President Trump failed to offer a clear Campaign Agenda or frame the election during his 2020 presidential re-election bid. He started with the Agenda of "Keep America Great," but stopped when the COVID-19 pandemic hit, the economy plunged, and a series of crises, including protests against racial injustice, erupted. *The Washington Post* noted that "The struggle to define Trump's reelection effort is a sharp departure from his first campaign for president," and quoted a former White House official as saying, "I don't know what their core message is right now… This is a big issue because if you go back to 2016, the main strength of the Trump campaign was a consistent message."

Six months before the election, *The Wall Street Journal* Editorial Board exclaimed, "As of now Mr. Trump has no second-term Agenda, or even a message beyond four more years of himself." In July 2020, Republican political consultant Karl Rove claimed in *The Wall Street Journal*, "If the President won't offer voters an agenda for his second term, he may not get one."

While Democratic challenger former Vice-President Joe Biden did not consistently repeat a single, clear Campaign Agenda, he ultimately landed on a "Battle for the Soul of America" Agenda that successfully framed the election as a referendum on President Trump's character and his failed response to the COVID-19 pandemic. Following Biden's victory, Rove wrote in a *WSJ* opinion, "Mr. Biden maneuvered successfully to make the election a referendum on the president's personality and his handling of COVID-19. For months, Mr. Trump was content to fight on that turf, trying only fitfully to contrast his agenda with his challengers."

The best political campaigns—and companies—use framing as a technique to convince voters or customers to see their candidacy or product in precisely the way they want them to see it.

## CHAPTER 3 SUMMARY

- *Force competitors to play your game.* The concept of "Create the Agenda" can also be thought of as "Play Your Game," since companies that play their game usually win the game. Donald Trump won the 2016 presidential election by forcing Hillary Clinton to play his game and follow his four-word Campaign Agenda of "Make America Great Again."
- *If you have more than one Agenda, then you have none.* Hillary Clinton used seven different Campaign Agendas over the course of her 2016 presidential run; she confused her voters and, in effect, competed against six other versions of herself.
- Traditionalist companies communicate numerous brand mes-

sages that are targeted to different customer segments. They believe *more is more*. In contrast, Transcender companies communicate one overarching Campaign Agenda, supported by two or three short C-Messages, to all their stakeholders. They believe **less is more**.

- **Transcenders do not necessarily need to have the most resources, largest marketing budget, or biggest sales force to win.** In fact, Transcenders often spend dramatically less on brand advertising and promotions than do Traditionalist companies.

- "Cognitive framing" is the lens through which humans unconsciously view their world. Transcender companies leverage the powerful framing effect to ensure their customers and stakeholders view the competitive marketplace through their specific lens.

# CHAPTER 4

## The Three Techniques to Create the Agenda

The first step in the Transcender System is Create the Agenda. Any one of three techniques can be used to Create the Agenda: *Competitive Creation, Competitive Re-Creation, and Competitive Categorization.* I will use a case study of Apple to describe and illustrate these three approaches.

### CASE STUDY: APPLE'S "THINK DIFFERENT" CORPORATE CAMPAIGN AGENDA

Steve Jobs co-founded Apple Computer (now known as Apple) in 1976 but was ousted from the company in 1985 following a corporate power struggle. However, over the next 12 years, it was the company that struggled: by 1997, Apple had dropped out of the top five companies in global personal computer sales for the first time and suffered its worst quarter ever, with a $700 million loss. The company was hemorrhaging money and had not had a breakthrough product in years. *LowEndMac.com* proclaimed that Apple "had shed the image of David to IBM's (or Microsoft's) Goliath. Apple was a tired company with tired products and boring leaders." The situation had become so dire that the board of directors brought back Jobs as CEO.

When Jobs first returned to his job, he told his staff: "It's a very noisy world. And we're not going to get a chance to get people to remember much about us. No company is. And so we have to be really clear on what we want them to know about us… Our customers want to know who is Apple and what is it that we stand for." As a Transcender leader, Jobs recognized that he needed two things: a winning Campaign Agenda and winning product candidates. While his team set out to create novel products, Jobs set out to find an advertising agency that could create a winning Campaign Agenda. He ultimately selected TBWA\Chiat\Day.

The advertising agency recommended the slogan "Think Different." Jobs insisted on the wording "Think Different" instead of the more commonly used "Think Differently" because the slogan did not tell someone how to think, but rather what to think. This was classic Jobs: thinking in entirely original ways not only with his products but also with his company's Campaign Agenda.

To support this Agenda, Apple's agency team created a two-minute commercial showcasing icons of the 20th century such as Alfred Einstein, Martin Luther King, Jr., Muhammad Ali, Amelia Earhart, and Pablo Picasso as change agents. The last two lines of the commercial were "*Because the people who are crazy enough to think they can change the world, are the ones who do.*"

Significantly, this commercial did not mention or show the Mac computer brand. This is the classic Transcender approach:

Apple led with its Campaign Agenda, not its product. If someone watching resonates with the idea that they, too, see things "different" and identify as a nonconformist, then they will be moved to buy an Apple Mac computer as a testament to their commitment to, and adoption of, the belief system "Think Different."

This ad campaign was effectively provocative and ultimately won numerous advertising awards. However, it was more than a simple advertising campaign—it became a corporate rallying cry. The two words Think Different became the corporate Campaign Agenda that helped catalyze the commercialization of three game-changing products: the iPod, the iPhone, and the iPad. Below is my representation of Apple's overarching Corporate Campaign Platform for these three iconic products:

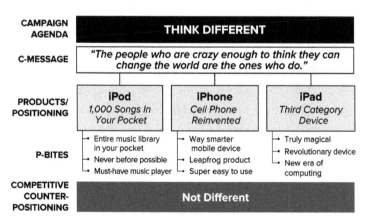

## Corporate Campaign Platform: Apple/Product Portfolio

| CAMPAIGN AGENDA | THINK DIFFERENT | | |
|---|---|---|---|
| C-MESSAGE | *"The people who are crazy enough to think they can change the world are the ones who do."* | | |
| PRODUCTS/ POSITIONING | **iPod** *1,000 Songs In Your Pocket* | **iPhone** *Cell Phone Reinvented* | **iPad** *Third Category Device* |
| P-BITES | → Entire music library in your pocket → Never before possible → Must-have music player | → Way smarter mobile device → Leapfrog product → Super easy to use | → Truly magical → Revolutionary device → New era of computing |
| COMPETITIVE COUNTER- POSITIONING | Not Different | | |

Note that this Campaign Platform is structurally different from President Obama's Campaign Platform. While both have an overarching Campaign Agenda and C-Messages, this one includes multiple products/franchises (e.g., the current iPhone and the iPhone franchise) while Obama was the only "product" or "brand" in his Campaign Platform. This Apple Campaign Platform is what I call a *Multi-Level Campaign Platform*" to distinguish it from Obama's one-level Campaign Platform.

This distinction is important: in the Transcender System, many companies conduct "**Multi-Level Competition.**" They may compete at four different levels: the *brand* level (e.g., the current iPhone product); the *franchise* level (the entire iPhone franchise, including previous and current iPhone models); the *portfolio* level (Apple's entire portfolio of products), and the *corporate* level (the perception of Apple as a corporation by its employees, customers, and stakeholders).

Most companies seek to compete on the level, or levels, that best provide a competitive advantage. For example, Apple prefers to compete at two levels: the corporate level, with its "Think Different" Agenda; and the brand level, with a focus on the newest-generation product in each of its franchises, while taking advantage of the popularity of previous product versions within the broader franchise. In contrast, Starbucks, which offers multiple coffee and grocery brands as well as several acquired food brands, prefers to compete primarily at the corporate level. In future chapters, I will share various case studies and examples of how companies use Multi-Level Competition differently.

I have used Apple as the first Transcender case study because these three Apple products perfectly illustrate the three ways companies can Create the Agenda. As shown below, the iPod, in combination with iTunes, illustrates "Competitive Creation": a product that creates an entirely new space. The iPhone demonstrates "Competitive Re-Creation": creating a game-changing product by reimagining an existing product, the cellphone. The iPad exemplifies "Competitive Categorization": owning a new, third category of device between the cellphone and the computer.

When a company like Apple has multiple products, each of their key products has its own Positioning and its own set of two or three "P-Bites" (Product Bites). P-Bites replace traditional brand messaging because they are shorter and more memorable. For example, the iPad is positioned as a "Third Category Device" that is "truly magical," a "revolutionary device," and "ushers in a new era of computing."

## Three Techniques to Create the Agenda

| Three Techniques to Create the Agenda | Descriptions | Examples from Apple Products |
|---|---|---|
| 1. Competitive Creation | Create a New Space | iPod/iTunes ("1,000 Songs in Your Pocket") |
| 2. Competitive Re-Creation | Re-Create an Existing Product | iPhone ("Reinvent the Cell Phone") |
| 3. Competitive Categorization | Own a New Category | iPad ("Third Category Device" between Cell Phone and Computer) |

## HOW THE IPOD CREATED A TOTALLY NEW SPACE

The first way to Create the Agenda is called Competitive Creation: creating a totally new virtual market space, thereby changing the game for the entire industry. The *InvestingAnswers. com* dictionary literally identifies the iPod as the definition of a game changer: "When Apple introduced the iPod, the product was a game changer. It revolutionized the way in which music was purchased and consumed. Though other companies had already launched MP3 players, Apple's product had a more attractive design, a big marketing budget, and, most important, a music platform (iTunes) that virtually dictated how music would be distributed going forward."

Competitive Creation is the idea that companies create products that customers cannot even imagine. Steve Jobs was a brilliant product developer and marketer. When Jobs introduced the iPod in 2001, he simply stated, "iPod: 1,000 songs in your pocket." At that time, no one could have imagined such a breakthrough digital device. Jobs proclaimed, "This is a quantum leap because for most people, it's their entire music library. This is huge."

The iPod was a revolutionary innovation, the first device capable of holding an entire music library in an ultra-portable package. It offered breakthrough battery technology to provide 10 hours of continuous music playback. However, what truly set the iPod apart as a new digital device was its seamless pairing with the iTunes app, which enabled users to download virtually unlimited songs. No other MP3 music player came close to the iPod's innovative design and technology integration. As Jobs later proclaimed, the iPod "didn't just change the way we all listen to music; it changed the entire music industry." The website *CultofMac.com* proclaimed, "By 2007, [Apple] sold its

100 millionth iPod. That made it Apple's most popular product until the iPhone. The device helped drive the success of the iTunes Music Store, which became America's top music retailer."

Nearly two decades after the iPod launch, the iPod touch is the only dedicated music player Apple still sells. Ultimately, it was Apple's iPhone—launched six years after the first iPod, with the iTunes app built-in—that cannibalized most iPod sales. The iPhone represents the second way to Create the Agenda: Competitive Re-Creation.

## CASE STUDY: APPLE'S RE-CREATION OF THE CELLPHONE

In addition to creating a product consumers cannot even imagine, companies can reach Transcender status by enhancing an existing product. I refer to this approach as **Competitive Re-Creation**, the second way to Create the Agenda. When the Apple iPhone was first introduced in 2007, customers did not necessarily see the need for another cellphone, but Steve Jobs realized that there was a need for a better cellphone *experience*. As Jobs noted, "It's really hard to design products by focus groups. A lot of times, people don't know what they want until you show it to them."

The original telephone and the cellphone were primarily designed simply to enable someone to call, and receive calls from, another person. In complete contrast, the iPhone was a user-friendly, web-enabled *mobile application platform*. With it, users could make/take calls, email, browse, take photos, make videos, navigate, play music, and do countless other activities. Introducing the iPhone at Macworld 2007, Jobs explained: "What we want to do is make a leapfrog product that is way smarter than any mobile device has ever been, and super-easy to use. This is what iPhone is."

Jobs designed the iPhone to be the first touchscreen-interface smartphone with nearly unlimited uses: "Design is not just what it looks like and feels like. Design is how it works." According to award-winning designer Natasha Jen, Jobs "applied his way of design thinking, which is intuition, on people's desires and needs, rather than business needs."

In short, the iPhone made virtually everything easier; the combination of simplicity and applicability made the iPhone a game-changing and life-changing product. Horace Dediu, a mobile phone industry analyst, said, "[The iPhone] is so much more than a product. It is an enabler for change. It unleashed forces which we are barely able to perceive, let alone control. It changed the world because it changed us."

In 2015, Apple's annual iPhone sales reached $236 billion. To date, Apple has sold over 2.2 billion iPhones worldwide. The iPhone has become Apple's best-selling product, typically driving over half of Apple's sales and propelling the company in 2020 to become the first US corporation to exceed a market valuation of $2 trillion.

## CASE STUDY: APPLE'S COMPETITIVE CATEGORY CREATION AND OWNERSHIP

A company does not have to be the first to create a new market space or reimagine an existing product to win. To change the game, it is more important to *own* the new category, as was the case with Apple's iPad. According to *Business Insider*'s Julie Bort, there were at least a half dozen commercially available tablets marketed prior to the Apple iPad, beginning with the Linus Write-Top in 1987—23 *years* before the iPad. Two years later, GRiD Systems released the GRiDPad 1900, the first commercially successful tablet computer. In fact, Apple launched its own first "tablet," the MessagePad, in 1993. Beginning in 2000, rival Microsoft launched two tablets, the Microsoft Tablet and the Windows XP tablet, years before the iPad. In fact, many technology experts credit Microsoft with coining the term "tablet."

But Apple was the first to *own* the category with the launch of the iPad in 2010. When Steve Jobs introduced the iPad, he presented a picture of an iPhone and a MacBook laptop with a question mark between them and asked a simple question: "Is there room for a *third category* of device in the middle?" He continued, "What the world needed was a device in the middle that combined the best of both—something that was more intimate than a laptop and so much more capable than a smartphone."

In Apple's press release announcing the new iPad, Jobs stated that the "iPad creates and defines an entirely new category of devices that will connect users with their apps and content in a much more intimate, intuitive, and fun way than ever before." The iPad was at that time "thinner and lighter than any laptop or netbook" and offered unprecedented technology: a much larger iPhone user-friendly touchscreen; unlimited access to the Apple App store, including the new iBooks app; an improved version of iWork, the first desktop-class productivity suite; optional Wi-Fi; and a host of other features, many specifically designed for the iPad. Jobs called the iPad "a truly magical and revolutionary device."

According to *CultofMac.com*, the iPad was Apple's most successful new product category launch, selling over one million units in its first month (less than half the time it had taken Apple to sell that many iPhones), and over 25 million in the first year—more than all the previous tablet sales *combined*. In its first nine months on the market, the iPad gained 90 percent market share and generated $9.5 billion, making it one of the most successful consumer products ever launched. "We've just never had a product get off to this fast of a start," Jobs said.

*The Wall Street Journal* proclaimed, "The last time there was this much excitement over a tablet, it had some commandments written on it." By 2011, the iPad had overtaken the DVD player to become the hottest-selling consumer electronics device of all time. In 2014, *USA Today* named the iPad as one of the top five best-selling products of all time. Ten years later, global iPad annual sales have surpassed $25 billion and represent over one-third of the tablet market. To date, *over 360 million* iPads have been sold.

Apple did not create the tablet PC category, but they were the first to own it. According to Chris Deaver, a former Apple executive, "Once [Apple] enters a category with a simply elegant solution, they can start charting the course and owning that space."

In the next chapter, I will explain how Starbucks created its own game to dominate the world's coffee business.

# CHAPTER 4 SUMMARY

- The first step in the Transcender System is to "Create the Agenda." There are three techniques to Create the Agenda: 1) *Competitive Creation*, 2) *Competitive Re-Creation*, and 3) *Competitive Categorization*.
- Three iconic Apple products illustrate the three ways Transcender companies can Create the Agenda:
  - The *iPod*, in combination with the digital iTunes music system, illustrates **"Competitive Creation"**: a product that created an entirely new space.
  - The *iPhone* demonstrates **"Competitive Re-Creation"**: creating a game-changing product by reimagining an existing product (the cellphone); and
  - The *iPad* exemplifies **"Competitive Categorization"**: owning a new category of device between the cellphone and the computer.

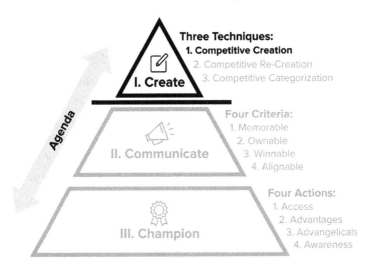

## The Transcender System

**Three Techniques:**
**1. Competitive Creation**
2. Competitive Re-Creation
3. Competitive Categorization

**I. Create**

**Four Criteria:**
1. Memorable
2. Ownable
3. Winnable
4. Alignable

**II. Communicate**

**Four Actions:**
1. Access
2. Advantages
3. Advangelicals
4. Awareness

**III. Champion**

Agenda

---

## CHAPTER 5

# Competitive Creation

If you recall, the first way to Create the Agenda is called Competitive Creation, which refers to creating a totally new virtual market space. Starbucks became the dominant coffee chain in the world by literally—and figuratively—creating a new space, "The Third Place" between home and work in America.

### CASE STUDY: STARBUCKS' CREATION OF A NEW SPACE

Co-founders Jerry Baldwin, Zev Siegl, and Gordon Bowker opened the first Starbucks in Seattle's historic Pike Place Market in 1971. For the first 16 years, Starbucks tried to win by playing the brand game. The company used the Starbucks brand name and an early version of their Nordic Siren brand logo. The founders tried to differentiate the brand based on its high-quality roasted coffee beans and brews. But the coffee chain was not winning. It was only adding one store per year.

In 1987, Howard Shultz bought the company and immediately changed Starbucks' branded coffee game to "The Third Place" between home and work in America. He explained to *Forbes* senior contributor Carmine Gallo: "*We are not in the coffee business...we're in the people business. It's all about the human experience... What I wanted to bring back was the daily ritual and the sense of community and the idea that we could build this third place between home and work in America.*"

Starbucks' goal was to become the Third Place in our daily lives: stop and linger at Starbucks on the way to work, or stop and linger at Starbucks on the way home. As Shultz envisioned it: "*You get more than the finest coffee when you visit Starbucks. You get great people, first-rate music, a comfortable and upbeat meeting place... At home, you are part of a family. At work you are part of a company. And somewhere in between there is a place where you can sit back and be yourself. That is what a Starbucks store is to many of its customers—a kind of 'Third Place' where they can escape, reflect, read, chat or listen.*"

As one Starbucks' store manager described it in a *Fast Company* article, "We want to provide all the comforts of your home and office. You can sit in a nice chair, talk on your phone, look out the window, surf the web...oh, and drink coffee too." Notice that she mentioned "drink coffee" last. In essence, traditional coffee shops want their customers to "grab a cup of coffee." Starbucks wants its customers to *grab a comfortable chair.*

Here is my overview of Starbucks' Campaign Platform:

## Starbucks Corporate Campaign Platform

| | |
|---|---|
| ***CAMPAIGN AGENDA***<br>*"Game" (≤5 words)* | **THE THIRD PLACE**<br>**(BETWEEN HOME AND WORK)** |
| ***CAMPAIGN C-MESSAGES***<br>*Concise communications to push the Campaign Agenda (3 max)* | • "We are not in the coffee business...we're in the people business. It's all about the human experience."<br>• "The idea behind customer service here is to make it one that isn't just good, we want to make it great."<br>• "We could build this 'Third Place' between home and work in America." |
| ***CAMPAIGN CANDIDATE***<br>*Company or Brand that best fits the Campaign Agenda* | **Starbucks** |
| ***CANDIDATE POSITIONING***<br>*Perception to be created for the Candidate in the minds of stakeholders (≤5 words)* | **The Third Place Experience** |
| ***COMPETITOR COUNTER-POSITIONING***<br>*Perception to be created for rivals in the minds of key stakeholders (<5 words)* | *All Other Competitors:*<br>*Just Coffee Shops* |

Note that Starbucks leads with the Campaign Agenda of The Third Place and then follows with the brand positioning of The Third Place Experience. Interestingly, Starbucks does not actively communicate its Agenda to the public at large. The vast majority of Transcender companies are *explicit* in repeatedly communicating their Campaign Agenda. In stark contrast, Starbucks uses an *implicit* Campaign Agenda approach: the company demonstrates rather than communicates its Campaign Agenda. Starbucks prefers customers to experience The Third Place rather than to tell them about it directly.

Notice first how Starbucks' Campaign Platform communications totally align with its Campaign Agenda; for example, Starbucks' three "C-Messages" (in quotations since they are actual corporate messages) support the novel concept of the company serving as "The Third Place between home and work in America." The Positioning of The Third Place Experience uses the same Campaign Agenda wording, The Third Place. This is a case of "Double Alignment": incorporating some of the wording of the Campaign Agenda into the Product Positioning.

Start with the Campaign Agenda and then determine the Product Positioning, since the Agenda *always* comes before the brand. The Product Positioning should fit the Agenda like a key into a lock. If a customer believes in Starbucks' Agenda, "The Third Place between home and work in America," then their stores must represent that so-called Third Place.

In this Campaign Platform, Starbucks is competing almost exclusively on the *corporate* level: Starbucks is the primary product or offering. The company does sell Starbucks-branded products (coffee, ice cream, and bottled cold coffee drinks) in grocery stores, and has acquired other brands, including Teavana tea products, Evolution Fresh juices, Frappuccino beverages, and La Boulange pastries. However, Starbucks continues to communicate its overarching Campaign Agenda as The Third Place because it does not want to compete as just another coffee shop.

However, it is not enough to Create and Communicate the Campaign Agenda; the best Transcender companies Champion the Agenda by aligning all their strategies, actions, activities, and measures to push the Campaign Agenda. Starbucks represents the archetype for this approach.

Nithin Geereddy, Vice President of Investment Strategy at J.P. Morgan, published a Harvard case study in 2014 that analyzed Starbucks' overall corporate strategy. Below I have briefly summarized one part of that analysis to show some of the winning Actions that Starbucks takes to support its The Third Place Agenda:

## ACCESS

- *Convenient Locations*: Starbucks strategically places its stores in heavily frequented corporate and suburban areas, including office buildings, transportation hubs, and retail centers. It is not unusual to see two Starbucks shops on opposite sides of a highway—one for on the way to work, one for on the way home.
- *Global Footprint and Large Size*: Starbucks has over 31,000 stores, spread across 80 countries, making them readily accessible. The stores are intentionally larger than other coffee shops to provide room for patrons' workspace and their guests.

## ADVANTAGES

- *Comfortable Community Spots and In-Store Experience*: Starbucks designs its stores to be welcoming, warm hangouts with comfortable chairs and couches, free Wi-Fi, a selective music playlist, and a stress-free, casual vibe.
- *Human Resources Management and Unique Corporate Culture*: To make its customers feel at home, Starbucks hires, trains, compensates, and treats its employees very well. The company offers stock options, typically reserved only for executives, and health care benefits even to part-time workers.

Unlike most Traditionalist companies, Transcender Starbucks spends more on employee training than on brand advertising. When partners start their job, the company provides them with the Starbucks Green Apron Book (named because it fits in a Green Barista Apron), which outlines their critical role in providing customers with superior service. Starbucks' US President Jim Alling refers to it as the "core ways of being" for success at Starbucks: be welcoming, genuine, knowledgeable, considerate, and involved. Starbucks' emphasis on training and treating their staff well leads to their staff treating its customers well.

- *Sophisticated Technology*: Starbucks leverages artificial intelligence and many other cutting-edge technologies to personalize and enhance "The Third Place Experience" in the front and back of the store. Starbucks uses machine learning to anticipate customers' preferences whether they are in-store, in their car, or on their Starbucks app. According to its technology partner Microsoft, the company deploys "reinforcement learning technology to analyze and offer its Starbucks Reward customers personalized food and drink suggestions on the app, based on their prior orders, local store inventory, popular selections, weather, time of day, and community preferences." Gerri Martin-Flickinger, Starbucks Executive Vice President and Chief Technology Officer, says, "Everything we do in technology is centered around the customer connection in the store, the human connection, one person, one cup, one neighborhood at a time." Starbucks seeks to provide a transcendent store experience.

## ADVANGELICALS/AWARENESS

- *Customer Loyalty*: Starbucks builds customer loyalty through The Third Place Experience approach by openly welcoming patrons and personalizing their visit. The Starbucks Rewards Program offers free food and drinks (including refills), the coffee industry's first phone payment app, birthday treats, and its highly popular "Stars" for purchases and visits.

Starbucks also uses a variety of unique promotions to create buzz, most notably its "Red Cup Campaign." Started in 1997 to build business during the holiday season, Starbucks annually creates and uses a unique, celebratory version of their holiday "red cup" in contrast to their standard green cup. According to *BigCommerce*, "The cups not only welcomed the arrival of the festive season but signify the beginning of Starbucks' holiday menu—including novel flavors such as 'Pumpkin Spice' latte. In this way, the campaign repeats annually, remaining fresh by adding new designs and drink flavors every year, and even inspiring similar campaigns from rivals such as Dunkin' Donuts." Notice how competitors must *react* to Starbucks.

- *Positive Impact and Corporate Responsibility*: As an embedded member of its The Third Place communities, Starbucks seeks to be a model citizen and give back locally. According to its *2020 Starbucks Global Environmental and Social Impact*

*Report*, Starbucks promotes sustainability and strengthens communities. For example, the company has focused on having "greener" stores, packaging, and cups, including a new "strawless lid" that helps reduce plastic straw usage by 70 percent. The company uses greater than 95 percent ethically sourced coffees and teas, while investing in tree reforestation and farmer loans.

Starbucks prides itself on its commitment and dedication "to creating and investing in opportunities for people around the world." Through its partnership with Feeding America, the company has contributed millions of fresh, unsold meals to local food banks. The Starbucks Foundation has also provided grants to the Opportunity for All organization to help build schools in developing countries.

- *Global Brand Awareness*: The Starbucks brand name, logo, and cups are recognized around the world. They signal to patrons the high standard of the Third Place Experience and premium products that a customer can expect in every Starbucks store. Like all other types of winning Actions, the Starbucks brand *supports* its overall Campaign Agenda.

Starbucks does not win by playing the Traditionalist brand game. For example, the company does not leverage brand advertising nearly as much as its rivals. Its primary competitor, Dunkin Donuts, typically spends twice as much in the US on advertising as Starbucks, yet Starbucks typically generates three times the coffee sales. Starbucks did not even start its first global advertising campaign until 2014, 18 years after it had entered the international market. Importantly, branding is a form of Awareness that certainly helps Transcenders win, but it is *not* the primary reason or way they win.

When McDonald's and other rivals attacked Starbucks in 2008, using traditional advertisements targeting its premium, high-priced coffees, Starbucks Chief Marketing Officer Terry Davenport told analysts, "We are not going to get sucked into the 'My coffee is better than your coffee' price point type of coffee conversation. We are going to play at a much higher level... We're going to keep doing what we do, and we're going to keep doing it our way." Starbucks has *transcended* competitors by refusing to play the conventional coffee game and focuses solely on playing its own game.

When Shultz acquired Starbucks in 1987, the company had a total of 17 stores. Over the next 20 years, Shultz aggressively expanded the number of stores, from one store per year to *1,350* stores per year. This is what I refer to as the "Transcendent Takeoff." In my consulting engagements, I have seen many times that when companies switch from a Traditionalist brand game to a Transcender Agenda game, they often experience a quantum leap in their competitive measure(s), including huge increases in sales, market share, or—in this case—number of coffee shops. This rocket takeoff is radically different from the more typical airplane trajectory of Traditionalist companies.

Ultimately, Shultz successfully steered Starbucks to carve out its own distinct space and play a game only it could win: to become The Third Place between home and work. By the time Schultz left Starbucks after his second stint as CEO in 2017, the company had grown to 27,339 stores worldwide.

Starbucks now operates more than 31,000 locations worldwide, serving 100 million customers per week in over 80 countries, meaning Starbucks has expanded far beyond Shultz's original premise of being "The Third Place Between Home and Work in America." By leveraging the Competitive Creation approach, Starbucks became the world's largest coffee chain, with nearly three times the number of coffee shops as its next biggest competitor, Dunkin' Donuts.

Reflecting on his original Campaign Agenda at Starbucks, Shultz wrote in 2018, "Providing the world with a warm and welcoming Third Place may just be our most important role and responsibility. Today and always." Clearly, Starbucks seeks to do all it can to communicate, demonstrate, and align with its Campaign Agenda of The Third Place.

I will describe in the next chapter how Peloton transcends its competitors by re-creating the cycling studio experience at home.

## CHAPTER 5 SUMMARY

- The first way to Create the Agenda, Competitive Creation, involves creating a totally new virtual market or "space."
- Starbucks literally and figuratively created a new space: the comfortable, convenient, and welcoming **Third Place** between home and work in America. Starbucks CEO Howard Shultz was *not* interested in playing the conventional brand coffee game. Starbucks created its own distinct space, played a game only it could win, and now dominates the global coffee market with over 31,000 stores, almost three times the size of its nearest competitor.
- Transcenders like Starbucks Champion the Agenda, winning by aligning all their communications and actions to push the Campaign Agenda.

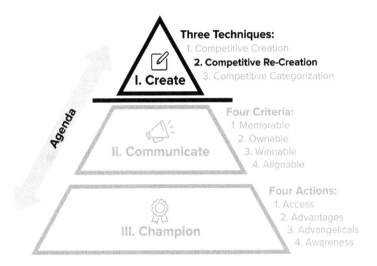

# The Transcender System

**Three Techniques:**
1. Competitive Creation
**2. Competitive Re-Creation**
3. Competitive Categorization

**I. Create**

**Four Criteria:**
1. Memorable
2. Ownable
3. Winnable
4. Alignable

**II. Communicate**

**Four Actions:**
1. Access
2. Advantages
3. Advangelicals
4. Awareness

**III. Champion**

Agenda

## CHAPTER 6

# Competitive Re-Creation

### CASE STUDY: PELOTON'S RE-CREATION OF THE CYCLING STUDIO EXPERIENCE

Just as Apple re-created the telephone, Peloton re-created the indoor fitness class cycling experience—complete with a totally new bike design, new apps, and a new cult following. Just as most people did not know they needed a different cellphone experience, most people also did not know they needed a different type of cycling class. According to *CNBC*'s Tom Huddleston, Jr., "Peloton was founded in 2012 to create a new concept in fitness. The founding team loved cycling but had a hard time finding a workout that consistently fit with their busy schedules, and at-home workouts never felt quite as good as a class. They set out on a mission to create a world-class indoor cycling studio experience that would rival the in-class experience—all from the comfort of home."

"We did talk a lot about Apple early on, and we talked about Netflix and Amazon," Tom Cortese, one of Peloton's five co-founders and COO, said. "When you think about these game-changer companies who have this focus on user experience, that is where we looked for inspiration." It all started with the bike itself. To reimagine fitness, the founders paid attention to every detail. They designed the Peloton bike with modern technologies, including a near-silent belt drive system and a smooth magnetic resistance flywheel; carbon steel construction for incredible strength and stability; and a cleverly constructed, easily gripped handle knob.

But designing the ultimate home exercise bike was just the start. Peloton had to reinvent the in-class experience. They added three important components: a first-in-class, 21.5-inch, full-HD, multi-touch console that connected to home Wi-Fi to deliver live and on-demand studio cycling classes; dynamic, professional cycling instructors who have gained cult followings; and a uniquely shared riding experience. The company's commitment to a shared experience—and to winning—is exemplified in its name: the French word "peloton" refers to the lead group in a professional bike race, such as the Tour de France.

To recreate that studio experience, Peloton added an integrated camera and microphone on the bike console, which enabled riders to compete with, video chat, motivate, and virtually high-five fellow cyclists. "We've also built a socially engaging platform in the workouts themselves," said Robin Arzon, Peloton's head instructor and vice president of fitness programming. "Whether you are getting a high-five from a fellow rider or getting a shout-out on your first run…there is an intimacy there that does not exist in most places, certainly not in a space where you are interacting digitally, and instructors are kind of breaking that fourth wall and in people's homes. That's really powerful stuff." Moreover, the Peloton bike tracks a rider's performance measures (e.g., total calories burned, distance, power outage) and progress, further encouraging riders to compete and achieve their fitness goals.

Here is my version of Peloton's *original* Corporate Campaign Platform:

## *Initial* Peloton Corporate Campaign Platform

| CAMPAIGN AGENDA<br>*"Game"* (≤5 words) | **WORLD-CLASS INDOOR CYCLING STUDIO EXPERIENCE** |
|---|---|
| *CAMPAIGN C-MESSAGES*<br>*Concise communications to push the Campaign Agenda (*<u>*3*</u> *max)* | • "Peloton's mission is to bring immersive and challenging workouts into people's lives in a more accessible, affordable, and efficient way."<br>• Peloton "creates a world-class indoor cycling studio experience that would rival the in-class experience — all from the comfort of home."<br>• Peloton offers "game-changing cardio you can't get enough of." |
| *CAMPAIGN CANDIDATE*<br>*Company or Brand that best fits the Campaign Agenda* | **Peloton** |
| *CANDIDATE POSITIONING*<br>*Perception to be created for the Candidate in the minds of stakeholders (≤5 words)* | **The Peloton Experience** |

The Peloton Campaign Agenda contains five words, which is within the three- to five-word memory recall range of most adults. This Campaign Platform illustrates Double Alignment: Peloton's Campaign Agenda and Positioning both use the word "experience." If a customer wants a World-Class Indoor Cycling Experience, Peloton is the company that offers it.

Importantly, Peloton is <u>not</u> competing primarily against other home fitness equipment companies; it is competing against health clubs and fitness studios by re-creating—and in many ways enhancing—the fitness studio experience. As CEO John Foley explained to *LinkedIn* Editor-in-Chief Dan Roth, "Four out of five Peloton bike buyers were not in the market for fitness equipment. So, we're not effectively selling fitness equipment, we're selling fitness. People want to be fit. They want fun, effective, convenient fitness experiences from their home. And that is what we provide them. And nobody else provides them, so we are kind of a category of one when you think about where we're taking our business." Peloton is playing a game only it can win.

During their 2020 Investor and Analyst Session, Peloton executives proclaimed that they were seeking to "digitally disrupt" the global fitness industry, which consists of over 36,500 health clubs and boutique fitness operators, by providing "better experiences, more selection, and time-shifted consumption at a better location (home)," thereby "rendering brick and mortar locations inferior." Peloton effectively changed the game by changing the competitive measure from the relatively high *equipment cost* of $2,500 for its Bike+ brand to the low *cost per workout*. "Think about yesteryear, when you would go pay $30 for a studio class, or $100 per month for a gym and maybe go 10 times—that's $10 per workout," CEO John Foley says. "Whereas right now, Peloton is seeing an average of about 25 workouts per [$39] subscription per month, which translates to about $1.60 per workout, at a better location, with better hardware and better instructors."

Peloton has created both a fitness phenomenon and an ardent cult following. It has been successful by any number of measures:

- To date, Peloton has sold over 400,000 bikes and has an estimated registered 1.4 million subscribers. This is despite the bike's relatively high price of approximately $2,500 per Bike+, excluding delivery and monthly fees. Annual global sales (including all exercise equipment sales, such as Peloton treadmills) are projected to be almost $4 billion in 2021.

- The company completed its initial public offering in September 2019, and already commands a market capitalization of over $32 billion.
- Peloton has over 800,000 social media followers, many of whom have shared their love of their Peloton bikes and experiences via word-of-mouth.

Peloton has added the "Peloton Tread" or treadmill on the same Peloton cycling app, as well as strength training, running, yoga, cardio classes, outdoor activities, meditation, stretching, and walking. The new Peloton Bike+, which debuted in 2020, is designed to take full advantage of these new streaming services.

In a 2020 *Wall Street Journal* interview, Foley said, "We plan to be the global digital fitness technology platform that allows you to work out at home and not have to travel." Like a politician, Foley is pivoting from Peloton's original Campaign Agenda of a "world-class indoor cycling studio experience" to its current Agenda of a "global digital fitness technology platform." This approach is different from having two different Agendas. The company is deliberately changing its Agenda as it grows beyond its initial bike offering. The company has recognized that it can be so much bigger than it originally believed. Transcenders think, act, and go big.

Peloton epitomizes the classic Transcender company that seeks not only to rise above its rivals but also to elevate its passionate followers. Foley has proclaimed that "Peloton is so much more than a bike—we believe we have the opportunity to create one of the most innovative global technology platforms of our time. It is an opportunity to create one of the most important and influential interactive media companies in the world; a media company that changes lives, inspires greatness, and unites people."

In the following chapter, I explore how Transcenders like Seedlip and Uber win by *owning* a new competitive category.

## CHAPTER 6 SUMMARY

- *Competitive Re-Creation* is the second of three ways to Change the Agenda. Like Apple's re-creation of the cellphone, Peloton re-created the indoor fitness class cycling experience—complete with a totally new bike design, new apps, and a new cult following.
- Peloton is not competing primarily against other home fitness equipment companies; it is taking on and transcending the much larger market of health clubs and fitness studios.
- When it launched the first Peloton bike, Peloton's original Corporate Campaign Agenda was "World-Class Indoor Cycling Studio Experience." As it added the Peloton Tread and other fitness apps, the company effectively expanded beyond this cycling-focused Agenda to a broader "Global Digital Fitness Technology Platform" Agenda.
- Peloton epitomizes the classic Transcender company that seeks not only to rise above its rivals but also to elevate and inspire its passionate followers.

# The Transcender System

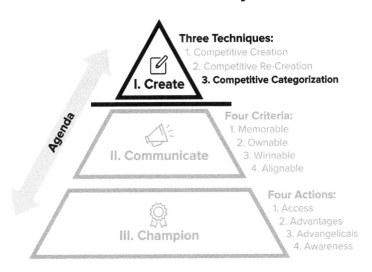

**Three Techniques:**
1. Competitive Creation
2. Competitive Re-Creation
3. **Competitive Categorization**

I. Create

Four Criteria:
1. Memorable
2. Ownable
3. Winnable
4. Alignable

II. Communicate

Four Actions:
1. Access
2. Advantages
3. Advangelicals
4. Awareness

III. Champion

Agenda

## CHAPTER 7

# Competitive Categorization

The third way to Change the Agenda is Competitive Categorization: creating or owning a new category of products, as Apple did with the iPad. Ideally, companies establish a new category in which their product is the only option. "Positive Competitive Categorization" highlights how your product is better (newer, next generation, distinct, etc.), while "Negative Competitive Categorization" highlights how a competitive product is worse (older, earlier generation, part of a flawed *status quo*).

There are several advantages to being the first to create a new category: defining the category on the company's terms, having first-mover advantage, shaping customers' perceptions of rivals as part of another "inferior" category, and creating a new market. Category creators demonstrate dramatically faster growth and higher valuations than their counterparts who only bring incremental innovations to market. The recent startup Seedlip typifies the benefits of being the first in a new category.

## CASE STUDY: SEEDLIP CREATES NEW CATEGORY OF DISTILLED NON-ALCOHOLIC SPIRITS

What happens if you mix a 370-year-old alcohol distillation book, a nine-generation family of farmers, and a design agency executive? The world's first distilled non-alcoholic spirits. Ben Branson was just trying to get a decent non-alcoholic drink on a Saturday night in London in 2013 when he encountered a bad mocktail. He said, "I was sick of drinking tonic water on its own and I didn't want to order a Shirley Temple with umbrellas and cherries hanging off it... I wanted to solve the dilemma of what to drink when you're not drinking—a good grown-up, sophisticated alternative."

Intrigued, Branson came across a pdf version of the book *The Art of Distillation*, originally published in 1651 by English physician John French. This book featured 42 woodcuts of the "choicest spagyrical preparations": herbal recipes for preparing non-alcoholic medical remedies distilled in copper stills. Branson sought out the original copy owned by King George III and bequeathed to the British Museum. He ultimately acquired his own copy, dated 1664, from an antique book dealer.

Fascinated by this book, and with a family background in farming, Branson bought his own copper still on the Internet and experimented with distilling home-grown herbs to create the first non-alcoholic spirits. He spent the next two years in his kitchen, fine-tuning his concoctions with various herbs, spices, and vegetables, including rosemary, thyme, peas, and hay.

Two years later, Branson had his first customer before he even had his first labeled bottle. He sold the idea, along with a few samples of his first distilled, non-alcoholic spirit, to a buyer at the iconic, high-end department store Selfridges in London. The buyer then introduced him to the five best bartenders in London. Branson was on his way to starting his company Seedlip, named after the farming baskets his family, generations earlier, had used to plant seeds. According to *Seedlip.com*, Branson "launched *Seedlip Spice 94* in London's Selfridges on November 4, 2015. His first 1,000 handmade bottles sold out within three weeks, the second 1,000 in three days, and the third in 30 minutes online."

Branson's timing represented a perfect storm: there was a demand for healthier, low-sugar drinks, but there were few available non-alcoholic alternatives. According to the company, "Seedlip is on a mission to change the way the world drinks with the highest quality non-alcoholic options." Note that the company is "on a mission" as opposed to having a "mission statement." I will discuss later how this mindset is typical of Transcender companies.

Branson effectively used Competitive Categorization to identify and own a third category of beverages between alcohol and soft drinks. Branson said, "We're challenging the industry, both the alcohol industry and the soft drinks industry, by trying to find our own way in the middle, to find this grey area that we want to occupy in this category that we're building. This will hopefully spark debate which encourages hotels, bars, and restaurants to think about their non-alcoholic offering more seriously." Calling Seedlip a "game-changer," *Forbes Magazine* in 2019 said, "Founder and teetotaller Ben Branson, 36, has broken through against the odds, by pioneering a new category of nonalcoholic drinks for adults, 'distilled non-alcoholic spirits.'"

According to Branson, "New categories often initially don't make sense the first time you hear them. Electric cars, dairy free milk—even mobile phones and online shopping were huge contradictions to what we had always known before. What we are doing with Seedlip is no different."

Here is my summary of Seedlip's Corporate Campaign Platform:

## Seedlip Corporate Campaign Platform

| | |
|---|---|
| **CAMPAIGN AGENDA**<br>*"Game" (≤5 words)* | **WORLD'S FIRST DISTILLED NON-ALCOHOLIC SPIRITS** |
| **CAMPAIGN C-MESSAGES**<br>*Concise communications to push the Campaign Agenda (3 max)* | • "Seedlip is on a mission to change the way the world drinks with the highest quality non-alcoholic options."<br>• Seedlip is "pioneering a new category of non-alcoholic drinks for adults, 'distilled non-alcoholic spirits.'"<br>• Seedlip is "offering a solution to the problem of 'what to drink when you're not drinking.'" |
| **CAMPAIGN CANDIDATE**<br>*Company or Brand that best fits the Campaign Agenda* | **Seedlip** |
| **CANDIDATE POSITIONING**<br>*Perception to be created for the Candidate in the minds of stakeholders (≤5 words)* | **The Distilled Non-Alcoholic Spirits Company** |

Like Peloton's Platform, Seedlip exemplifies Double Alignment: the company's positioning uses the same wording as the Campaign Agenda. The company's initial marketing slogan was "What to drink when you are not drinking." A marketing slogan often can be used as a C-Message to help communicate the Campaign Agenda.

Branson used a twofold strategy to create awareness for his brands. First, he used "old-fashioned shoe leather," pounding the pavement to talk directly with the world's leading bartenders, a relatively small but highly influential group of about 500 global professionals who regularly communicate with one another. He believed that "if the best bartenders supported Seedlip brands, then we had a chance." Second, he focused on getting "earned press": telling the media a unique, "first-of-its-kind story that wants to be shared." As a Transcender, Branson knew that earned (free) media was much more influential and authentic than promotional (paid) media, more commonly used by Traditionalists.

In the process, Branson has helped to start a movement for "normality and social acceptance" of people who do not drink alcoholic beverages. He said his goal was to make sure no one walks into a bar or a party and is uncomfortable because they do not drink.

Seedlip has exploded onto the market. The company currently markets three unique blends, is launching a new aperitif, and has more products in the pipeline. In less than four years, Seedlip has launched its three spirits into 25 countries and over 7,500 of the world's best bars, hotels, retailers, and restaurants, including 300 Michelin Star restaurants. Despite the presence of over 50 competitive brands, Seedlip currently commands a 70 percent share of the non-alcoholic spirits global market.

As a result of this tremendous success, the Diageo Corporation, a global leader in alcoholic beverages and producer of Guinness, Smirnoff, and more, announced in 2019 that it had acquired majority ownership in Seedlip, its first acquisition of a non-alcoholic beverage company in its 258-year history. John Kennedy—President of Diageo Europe, Turkey, and India—proclaimed that "Seedlip is a game-changing brand in one of the most exciting categories in our industry."

Branson was willing to partner with Diageo, the world's leading spirits company, because he believes that they represent the key to Seedlip winning in the future when there are hundreds of non-alcoholic spirits brands. He says Seedlip is "unleashing the power of Diageo" because they "have the power and influence to change the way the world drinks."

In contrast to Seedlip, Uber demonstrates that it is not necessarily who is first to market—rather, it is who is first to *own the market* that wins.

## CASE STUDY: UBER OWNS A THIRD NEW CATEGORY OF RIDESHARING SERVICES

Most people think of Uber first when they think about ridesharing services. However, Uber did not invent the ridesharing service business. Ridesharing started over 400 years ago when the first taxi service launched via horse and carriage in 1605 in Paris and London. The first automobile-based taxis ("yellow cars") arrived 300 years later. Limousines, a second category of ridesharing, were created in the French Provence of Limoges in 1902.

The third market category and the modern-day version of ridesharing—using an app to call for a shared ride—was first conceived by Sidecar co-founder and CEO Sunil Paul, who was the first to patent the idea in 2002. Paul, along with co-founders Jahan Khanna and Adrian Fortino, started Sidecar late in 2011. According to the San Francisco-based news website *SF Gate*, Sidecar started offering "peer-to-peer rides from people in their personal cars a year before Uber and Lyft." Fortino said at the time that "we're going to replace your car with your iPhone."

In a 2016 *DMNews* article entitled "How Uber Won The Rideshare Wars and What Comes Next," journalist Elyse Dupre explained that at that time, there were five different types of competitors vying to win the new ridesharing category: "There were the established self-drive, car-sharing players like Zipcar, which launched in 2000; the startups reimagining the black car experience (Uber); the startups looking to pair people together for long trips (Zimride, which became Lyft); the startups looking to build software to improve the taxi industry (GetTaxi, Cabulous); and the startups creating a whole new marketplace— where normal citizens could treat their cars as inventory and make money through providing rides to those in need (Sidecar)."

Uber co-founders Garrett Camp and Travis Kalanick had already launched their brand UberCab (later known as Uber) in 2009, but it had offered an app-based, on-demand black car luxury service featuring chauffeurs. In contrast, Sidecar offered a more casual, peer-to-peer model: riders would use an app to order pickups from drivers using their own cars.

According to Dupre, "Because their intended audiences were different, their approaches were different, too. Whereas Uber originally relied on chauffeurs to transport customers from point A to point B, Sidecar leveraged a peer-to-peer model... There was also a difference in branding. Uber focused on offering consumers a luxury, on-demand black car service, complete with high-end SUVs and sedans. Sidecar, contrastingly, focused on providing a friendly, more informal experience—asking drivers to use their own cars to tote around other passengers and invite their guests to sit in the front seat." Notice that Uber originally focused on product branding, while Sidecar emphasized the ridesharing *experience*.

According to Harry Campbell, founder of the blog *The Rideshare Guy,* "Sidecar had always been the first in rideshare. It was the first to offer on-demand rides, way before [Lyft co-founders] John Zimmer and Logan Green had even seen a pink mustache or Travis [Kalanick] had gone to Paris to think about how much taxi rides sucked. And as the battle for the market of drivers and passengers raged, Sidecar came up with all the cool technology Uber and Lyft are testing years later: destination filters, custom pricing, the ability to favorite a driver, back-to-back rides, and the ability for a passenger to select the driver they wanted from within the app."

However, rival Uber soon recognized the huge peer-to-peer model opportunity and jumped into the mass-market ridesharing category that Sidecar had initiated, launching UberX in 2012. Despite not being the first company in this category, Uber quickly became the new category leader and ultimately *owned* the ridesharing industry. To own the space, Uber leveraged the "four A's" of the Transcender System: *Access, Advantages, Advangelicals,* and *Awareness.*

*Access/Advantages:* Uber had several advantages over its rivals at the time, including dramatically more funding. This allowed it to recruit more drivers, thereby creating the best ridesharing access. Campbell said, "Uber definitely has the fastest pick-up times because they have the most drivers and the most riders." Sidecar's Fortino confirmed this when he said, "Uber has won because they consistently deliver the fastest pick-up time. That's because, in hindsight, they raised the most money. That money goes toward data science; it goes toward obviously driver adoption... To me, it's just a singular competitive dynamic: pick-up time. How quickly do I get picked up? That's it."

In addition, Uber dramatically enhanced its model to provide a superior rider experience, including simple booking via the Uber app; safe pickups by providing detailed driver information; various car options, such as UberX, UberXL, UberSELECT, and UberBLACK; lower fees than traditional taxis and limousines with cashless payments; and high-quality, professional drivers by vetting, training, and monitoring drivers through customer feedback and ratings.

*Advangelicals:* Uber encouraged avid supporters and early adopters by giving first-time riders free trials and rewarding riders who referred others. One "super-referrer" reportedly earned over $50,000 in referral credits. These advocates helped promote and spread the word for Uber. Early on, Uber introduced a rider loyalty program, initially called Uber VIP, which evolved into Uber Rewards. These programs rewarded riders based on the amount they spent on the platform and further built a devoted following.

*Awareness:* According to marketing solutions provider Annex Cloud, Uber created buzz through public relations stunts like "on-demand hot air balloon and boat rides, cuddle huddles with puppies and kittens, wine trips, Christmas tree tours, and helicopter rides." The company increased awareness by partnering with established players including Capital One, which offered its credit card holders discounted rides, and Starwood Hotels, which offered Preferred Guest members hotel points for Uber trips. Spotify users who link their profile to their Uber account can have their music list played while they ride. These types of partnerships increased awareness and helped to validate the company.

Importantly, all of Uber's Actions supported and aligned with its corporate Campaign Agenda of "Everyone's Private Driver." The company consistently communicated its initial, early Campaign Agenda and Platform, which I summarized below:

## *Initial* Uber Corporate Campaign Platform

| | |
|---|---|
| **CAMPAIGN AGENDA**<br>*"Game" (≤5 words)* | **EVERYONE'S PRIVATE DRIVER** |
| **CAMPAIGN C-MESSAGES**<br>*Concise communications to push the Campaign Agenda (3 max)* | • "Uber is the smartest way to get around."<br>• "Tap the app, get a ride."<br>• "The one-stop shop and operating system for modern city life." |
| **CAMPAIGN CANDIDATE**<br>*Company or Brand that best fits the Campaign Agenda* | **Uber** |
| **CANDIDATE POSITIONING**<br>*Perception to be created for the Candidate in the minds of stakeholders (≤5 words)* | **Undisputed Global Leader in Rides** |

Uber has become a business behemoth, literally changing the lexicon: fewer people are "calling a taxi" and more are "taking an Uber" (or just "Ubering"). In a *Growth Hackers* post, Sean Ellis, Everette Taylor, and Dylan la Com said that "Uber set out to reimagine the entire [taxi] experience to make it seamless and enjoyable across the board. Uber didn't fix one aspect of the system (e.g., mobile payments for the existing taxi infrastructure), they tackled the whole experience from mobile hailing,

seamless payments, better cars, to no tips, and driver ratings."
Uber created a more transcendent ride experience and ultimately owned the new ridesharing category that others had
created.

Over the past decade, Uber has grown dramatically and has
leveraged its massive technology platform to enter many other
businesses. Each of its respective brands has its own Positioning that ladders up to the company's new Campaign Agenda
of "Setting the World in Motion," as shown in the illustrative
current Uber Campaign Platform below:

## *Current* Uber Corporate Campaign Platform: Uber/Product Portfolio

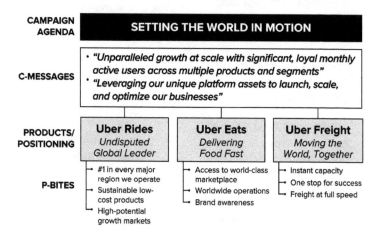

These newer product offerings currently include Uber Eats
(with the Positioning of Delivering Food Fast); Uber Freight
(Moving the World, Together); Uber for Business (Simplify-
ing How Your Business Gets Around); Advanced Technology
Group (The Road to Self-Driving Vehicles); Uber Elevate (The
Future of Urban Mobility, including drone deliveries); Uber

Health (Fewer No-Shows. More On-Time Appointments, which schedules rides for health appointments); and Uber New Mobility (JUMP Bikes and Scooters).

Across its multiple products and segments, Uber currently has $58 billion in total annual gross bookings, seven billion trips, and five million riders in over 10,000 cities across 69 countries. With a current valuation of over $107 billion, the company is worth more than General Motors, Ford, and Honda, three of the world's largest auto manufacturers. In January 2016, General Motors acquired the remaining assets and intellectual property of Sidecar, the company that founded ridesharing in its current form, which had ceased corporate operations in December 2015.

In the next chapter, I reveal the four criteria for effectively Communicating the Agenda.

## CHAPTER 7 SUMMARY

- The second technique to Create the Agenda is **Competitive Categorization**: creating or owning a new product category.
- Seedlip founder Branson successfully leveraged Competitive Categorization to pioneer a new category of distilled non-alcoholic spirits that fit between alcohol and soft drinks. Seedlip has become the dominant player in the category with a 70 percent share of the global market.
- Successful Competitive Categorization does not require initiating a new product category. Uber did not create but ultimately owned the ridesharing service category by leveraging Transcender approaches.

# COMMUNICATE
# THE AGENDA

# The Transcender System

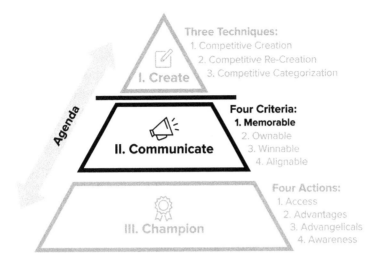

**Three Techniques:**
1. Competitive Creation
2. Competitive Re-Creation
3. Competitive Categorization

I. Create

Agenda

II. Communicate

**Four Criteria:**
1. **Memorable**
2. Ownable
3. Winnable
4. Alignable

III. Champion

**Four Actions:**
1. Access
2. Advantages
3. Advangelicals
4. Awareness

CHAPTER 8

# Memorable

Once you have created the Campaign Agenda, the next step in the Transcender System is to **Communicate the Agenda.** There are four criteria to use when evaluating the probable effectiveness of a Campaign Agenda:

1. *Memorable*: Is the Agenda easily remembered and recalled?
2. *Ownable*: Will my company be most closely associated with this Agenda?
3. *Winnable*: Will this Agenda help my company win versus rivals' Agendas?

4. *Alignable*: Can my company's professionals support and implement this Agenda? Can customers and other stakeholders believe in and communicate this Agenda?

I use the mnemonic **MOWA** to help remember these criteria. In the following four chapters, I will detail what I mean by Memorable; I will then discuss Ownable in Chapter 9, Winnable in Chapter 10, and Alignable in Chapter 11.

An effectively Memorable Campaign Agenda has five characteristics: it is *simple*, *distinct*, *repetitive*, *consistent*, and *visual*.

## 1. SIMPLE

As humans, we store information in our brains in two basic ways: with short-term memory and long-term memory. As the words suggest, short-term memory is temporary—basically what we are currently thinking about, while long-term memory allows us to remember a significantly greater amount of information for much longer.

Short-term memory has a limited capacity and decays rapidly. According to early memory research conducted by G.A. Miller in 1956, most adults at that time were able to remember 7 +/- 2 words or "chunks" of information in short-term memory for about 20-30 seconds at a time. However, more recent research by Dr. Nelson Cowan at the University of Missouri and others have revealed that US adults are now capable of remembering only 4 +/- 1 words or chunks of information in short-term memory. In a 2010 research paper entitled "The Magical Mystery Four: How is Working Memory Capacity Limited and Why," Cowan demonstrated that "there is an underlying limit on a central component of working memory, typically 3–5 chunks in young adults." This recent 43 percent loss in short-term memory capacity is likely exacerbated by two factors: our overreliance on our cellphones for remembering telephone numbers and other information, and the massive increase in the amount of information bombarding us every day.

**To remember something, it must be five words or fewer.** This finding is essential to understanding Transcender communications. **If you want something to get into long-term memory, it must first get into short-term memory. To get into short-term memory, it must be five words or fewer.**

For example, look at the winning slogans of first-term US presidents over the last 70 years:

- 1948: Harry Truman: *The Buck Stops Here*
- 1952: Dwight E. Eisenhower: *I Like Ike*
- 1960: John F. Kennedy: *A Time for Greatness*
- 1964: Lyndon Baines Johnson: *All the Way with LBJ*
- 1968: Richard Nixon: *This Time, Vote Like Your Whole Life Depended on It*
- 1976: Jimmy Carter: *A Leader, For a Change*
- 1980: Ronald Reagan: *Let's Make America Great Again*
- 1988: George H.W. Bush: *Kinder, Gentler Nation*
- 1992: Bill Clinton: *For People, For a Change (unofficial slogan: "It's the Economy, Stupid")*
- 2000: George W. Bush: *Compassionate Conservatism*
- 2008: Barack Obama: *Change*
- 2016: Donald Trump: *Make America Great Again*
- 2020: Joe Biden: *Battle for the Soul of America*

Every one of these presidential winners, except Nixon and Biden, had simple slogans that were five words or fewer. It is important to understand that not all slogans are necessarily Campaign Agendas. In some cases, the slogans are simply pithy, catchy terms that help people remember a candidate, while Campaign Agendas are the lens through which candidates want to frame the election. For example, "I like Ike" is a slogan, but not an Agenda. In this case, the slogan is leading with the candidate or "brand," not with the Campaign Agenda.

I generally encourage my clients to create four-word Agendas, because some people cannot remember even five words. Importantly, the fewer number of words, the easier it will be to memorize. Cowan refers to this as "maximum simplicity."

I use an elevator metaphor to help people remember the five-words-or-fewer concept. In the Traditionalist System, there was the "Elevator Speech": a sales professional bumping into a potential customer on an elevator would have several floors to give a 30-second elevator pitch about his product or company. In the Transcender System, we have the "**Elevator Close.**" Now, the professional has time to say only four words as the elevator door closes: "*Wait, hold the elevator!*" The concept of the Elevator Close is that if you can only communicate four words to your customer on an elevator, it should be the Campaign Agenda, since it is far more important to *Communicate the Agenda* than it is to promote the brand.

# Elevator Communications

**Traditionalist System:**
**"Elevator Speech"**

**Transcender System:**
**"Elevator Close"**

**30-Second Discussion:**
*Several Sentences*

**4-Word Close:**
*"Wait, Hold that Elevator!"*

Communicating simply can be a challenge. In a 1998 *Business Week* article, Steve Jobs stated, "That's been one of my mantras—focus and simplicity. Simple can be harder than complex: You have to work hard to get your thinking clean to make it simple. But it's worth it in the end because once you get there, you can move mountains."

For example, when Jobs introduced the iPod, he could have exclaimed, "The iPod is a 6.5-ounce, ultraportable digital music device with a razor-thin 5 GB hard-drive that can hold 1,000 songs and play continuously on 10 hours of battery life powered by its rechargeable lithium polymer battery which recharges automatically whenever iPod is connected to a Mac." Instead, Jobs simply said "1,000 songs in your pocket"—*five* words.

The best Transcender companies and professionals use five words or fewer for their Campaign Agenda, the Positioning of their products, their "P-Bites"—concise product bites that replace traditional brand messaging—and the Counter-Positioning of their competitors.

## 2. DISTINCT

Campaign Agendas that are distinct are much more likely to be remembered. For example, Bill Clinton's official Campaign Agenda in the 1992 presidential election was "For People, For a Change." However, people are much more likely to remember his *unofficial* Agenda of "It's the Economy, Stupid" because it is so unique. The story goes that Clinton's political strategist James Carville wanted to keep the campaign "on message," so he posted a sign at the Little Rock, Arkansas, campaign headquarters with that phrase. Although the sign was initially directed at his internal campaign team, this phrase focusing on the economy was more memorable and ultimately became the de facto Campaign Agenda for the successful Clinton election campaign.

Per Sederberg, a psychology professor at The Ohio State University and memory researcher, has found that novel or "peculiar" concepts are more likely to be remembered. "You have to build a memory on the scaffolding of what you already know, but then you have to violate the expectations somewhat. It has to be a little bit weird," Sederberg says.

## 3. REPETITIVE

A simple and distinct five-word Campaign Agenda is not enough to ensure people remember it, and, more importantly, repeat it to others—the goal of winning campaign communications. In the Traditionalist System, marketers are often pleased if their customers *recognize* their brand messages. In the Transcender System, business professionals want customers to *repeat* the Campaign Agenda (e.g., Change, Make America Great Again) to many other stakeholders. This is analogous to the difference between recognizing someone's face versus recalling and repeating their name.

To achieve this goal of stakeholders constantly repeating the Campaign Agenda, they must hear the Agenda numerous times. Repetition studies have shown that only repetitive communications of the Campaign Agenda will enable these stakeholders to recall and repeat the Agenda. Two-time US Memory Champion and Memory Training Expert Ron White explains:

*"Repetition [is] one of the keys to improving your memory... It reinforces the lesson in your brain and the more you repeat it the better you will remember. Once committed to memory it is not likely to be lost, even if that information is not utilized again for years."*

Importantly, *recalling* information dramatically enhances memory. As a young child, I reviewed spelling words over and over until they were hardwired into my brain. The more I used those words, the more often I recalled how to spell them, and the better those words became ingrained in my mind. Similarly, the more we recall previously learned information from long-term memory, the more it enhances our memory recall.

## 4. CONSISTENT

The key to memory recall is to retrieve the *same information* repeatedly. Therefore, the best politicians are consistent when they repeat their five-words-or-fewer Campaign Agenda. Consistency means saying the **exact same words** every single time. During the 2016 Election Campaign, President Trump never swayed from his precise four-word Campaign Agenda of Make America Great Again. He never said, "Let's Make the USA Great Again" or "Make America Better." He persistently and relentlessly said the same four words.

Similarly, Boris Johnson constantly and consistently repeated his

Campaign Agenda of "Get Brexit Done" during the Conservative Party's 2019 winning election campaign in the United Kingdom. The day after the December 11, 2019, election, *The Washington Post* reported that "the results of the United Kingdom's general election will not be announced for hours, but already an apparent winner has emerged among campaign slogans: 'Get Brexit Done.' That has been the No. 1 talking point of Prime Minister Boris Johnson and his Conservative Party through the six-week election campaign. He has cited it repeatedly. On Wednesday, he tweeted it more than 20 times and was back at it on Thursday morning. Earlier in the week, he broke through a foam wall with a bulldozer emblazoned with the phrase… As a result, when political focus groups are asked to shout out the first party slogan that comes to mind, people say: 'Get Brexit Done.'"

Rob Ford, a politics professor at the University of Manchester, claimed the Conservatives' "ruthless message discipline" was the deciding factor in the 2019 election. *Time* magazine went further: "'Get Brexit Done.' That was the slogan repeated on every billboard, pamphlet, and doorstep during the Conservative Party's campaign for the U.K. Election… And when the results came through overnight, it was clear those three words had helped win Boris Johnson's party an overwhelming majority… If you compare the two parties, the message discipline exercise[d] by the Conservative Party was incredibly impressive relative to the very diffuse, very confusing signaling coming out of the Labor Party."

Transcender professionals who adhere to *simple, distinct, repetitive*, and *consistent* product communications achieve significantly better stakeholder recall of, and belief in, their Campaign Agenda. This, in turn, ultimately leads to improved product sales.

## 5. VISUAL

To further enhance memorization of a Campaign Agenda, professionals rely on visuals such as pictures and images. The adage "a picture is worth a thousand words" has many ascribed origins, but it has been demonstrated in scientific research; the results are called the picture superiority effect. Simply put, humans are more likely to remember and recall information when it is presented in pictures or images (e.g., the photo of an elephant) than in words ("elephant"). According to presentation expert Marta Kagan, not only do humans remember visual content better, but they also process visual information 60,000 times faster in the brain than they do textual input. This is likely because pictures provide a literal representation while text symbolizes a figurative representation.

Politicians extensively leverage the picture superiority effect: presidential candidate Obama's supporters plastered his HOPE/CHANGE posters everywhere possible, while President Trump and his followers were almost universally seen wearing the red Make America Great Again (or "MAGA") hats. The best Transcender companies and communicators take the time to create and saturate their stakeholders with unique, memorable images, such as Apple's iconic bitten apple, Starbucks' Nordic Siren, and Nike's Swoosh logo.

Logos are certainly not new to the Transcender System; they are derived from ancient hieroglyphs, symbolism, and family crests. The initial forms are derived from the Middle Ages (around 1300 AD) when shops and pubs used signs to highlight their offerings. The first modern logo designs did not evolve until the early 1900s, when mass printing became available. Transcender companies effectively use their logos to align with and specifically *support* their Campaign Agendas.

For example, in 1971 Nike's founder Phil Knight asked Carolyn Davidson, one of his accounting students who also happened to be a graphic artist, to design a logo that "inspired movement." She produced several logos, including the Swoosh, a symbol inspired by the wings of the Greek Goddess of Victory Nike. This,image aligns perfectly with Nike's Campaign Agenda "Just Do It," which encourages people just to move. In the Transcender System, companies extensively use brand logos, but they are designed to create awareness for and reinforce the overall Campaign Agenda.

## CASE STUDY: GEICO'S MEMORABLE CAMPAIGN AGENDA

GEICO, a leading car and motorcycle insurer, is the prime example of how to communicate a memorable Campaign Agenda using the five attributes of simple, distinct, repetitive, consistent, and visual. Starting with its television commercials in 1999, GEICO proclaimed "15 minutes could save you 15% or more on car insurance." In Transcender terms, GEICO was communicating a simple, four-word Campaign Agenda of "15 Minutes, 15%," as I illustrate below:

## GEICO Insurance
## Corporate Campaign Platform

| | |
|---|---|
| **CAMPAIGN AGENDA**<br>*"Game" (≤5 words)* | **15 MINUTES, 15%** |
| **CAMPAIGN C-MESSAGES**<br>*Concise communications<br>to push the Campaign<br>Agenda (3 max)* | • "15 minutes could save you 15% or more on car insurance."<br>• "Everybody knows that."<br>• "So easy a caveman could do it." |
| **CAMPAIGN CANDIDATE**<br>*Company or Brand that best<br>fits the Campaign Agenda* | **GEICO Insurance** |
| **CANDIDATE POSITIONING**<br>*Perception to be created for<br>the Candidate in the minds<br>of stakeholders (≤5 words)* | **Easy Savings** |
| **COMPETITOR<br>COUNTER-POSITIONING**<br>*Perception to be created for<br>rivals in the minds of key<br>stakeholders (<5 words)* | *All Other Competitors:<br>Difficult, Costly* |

GEICO has relentlessly repeated the *same* Campaign Agenda in its online and offline advertising for over 20 years. What makes GEICO exceptional is how it communicates its Agenda. Unlike traditional advertising, GEICO runs different types of commercials at the same time. Moreover, the company has used as many as six different visual and distinct characters—ranging from its iconic Gecko to Cave Men and Pinocchio.

HawkPartners consultant Cynthia Herr published a GEICO analysis entitled "Three Ingredients for a Great Ad." She wrote,

"Not only is the message simple, but Geico has remained true to it over the years. Geico has leveraged one of the longest-running taglines and call-to-action strategies in history, resulting in a recall rate of 90%. The campaign may seem erratic; Geico has launched ad after ad, often with multiple ads at once. One day [the ads feature] camels, the next day collect calls, and the next day a pig hanging out a car window screaming 'wee, wee, wee' all the way home. And yet the core message has not changed; the tagline has never wavered. Keeping it fresh doesn't have to mean big changes; in fact, consistency in messaging can actually enable creativity and innovation." Importantly, virtually all of GEICO's ads consistently communicate and align with its core Campaign Agenda of "15 Minutes, 15%."

GEICO even pokes fun at its target audience: "So easy, a Caveman can do it." Other ads have stated, "15 minutes could save you 15% or more on car insurance. Everybody knows that." Why do we know it? Because GEICO has repeatedly and consistently been communicating the exact same Agenda for decades.

According to the advertising data company MediaRadar, GEICO spent $390 million on advertising during the first quarter of 2020, the highest of *any* company in the US. While this is atypical for Transcenders, GEICO is leveraging its unique advertising approach to compete with the leader, State Farm Insurance, which relies more heavily on promotions from its massive insurance broker network of 19,200 agents. Importantly, GEICO is using advertising in a way that directly supports and aligns with its Campaign Agenda.

According to Renee Quinn at *IPWatchdog*, a business intellectual property site, GEICO's initial advertising campaign strategy was to "saturate the market with print advertising, radio ads, and television advertisements..." Subsequently, the company has dramatically expanded its messaging across digital media. "No matter what channel you watch, what radio station you listen to or what newspaper and magazines you read, chances are there is at least one GEICO ad being used in that venue."

This level of repetition and consistency is often what separates Transcender winners from Traditionalist competitors. Most traditional marketers change their brand messaging routinely to ensure that customers do not experience brand fatigue. In contrast, GEICO has stayed with the same four-word Campaign Agenda consistently for the past two decades. For example, when car owners dramatically reduced their driving during the 2020 coronavirus pandemic, 11 of the biggest auto insurance companies offered one-time refunds, ranging from Nationwide's $50 premium refund to State Farm's 25 percent premium credit. What did GEICO offer? Exactly 15 percent credit, as always, consistent with GEICO's Campaign Agenda of "15 Minutes, 15%."

Later that same year, GEICO ran a commercial in which its Gecko explained the origin of "15 minutes, 15%." He claimed that he initially thought of a different slogan: "'In a quarter of an hour, your savings will tower.' But that's not catchy is it, and that's not going to swim about in your brain. So I thought, what about '15 minutes, 15%?'"

Over a 15-year period, GEICO's Transcender approach of repetitively and consistently communicating its simple Campaign Agenda catapulted the company from fifth to second among leading car insurance companies in America. GEICO is currently only two market share points behind and gaining on State Farm Insurance, which has the advantage of offering and bundling more types of insurance products, including life and health insurance.

The first criterion in Communicating the Agenda is to make it memorable; the next important criterion is to make it ownable.

## CHAPTER 8 SUMMARY

- Once you have created the Campaign Agenda, the next step is to **Communicate the Agenda**. Use four criteria when evaluating the probable effectiveness of a Campaign Agenda: it should be *Memorable, Ownable, Winnable*, and *Alignable*. I use the mnemonic **MOWA** to help remember these criteria.
- The first criterion is **Memorable**. There are five constituent elements of a Memorable Campaign Agenda: it is *simple, distinct, repetitive, consistent*, and *visual*. GEICO's two-decade-long "15 Minutes, 15%" campaign brilliantly illustrates all five.
  - *Simple*: **To remember something, it must be five words or fewer.** Research has revealed that humans can typically remember up to five words in their short-term memory, so Campaign Agendas should be five words or fewer.
  - *Distinct*: Campaign Agendas that are distinct are much more likely to be remembered. For example, Bill Clinton's official Campaign Agenda in the 1992 presidential election was For People, For a Change. However, people are much more likely to remember his unofficial Agenda of "It's the Economy, Stupid," because it is unique.
  - *Repetitive*: The goal of Transcender communications is not only to ensure that people *remember* the Campaign Agenda but that they also *repeat* it to others. In the Transcender System, we want stakeholders to repeat the Campaign Agenda (e.g., Change; Make America Great Again) to poten-

tial customers. To achieve this goal, they must hear the Agenda numerous times.

- *Consistent*: The key to memory recall is to retrieve the *same information* repeatedly. Consistency means communicating the *exact same words* of the Campaign Agenda every single time.
- *Visual*: To further enhance stakeholders' memorization of a Campaign Agenda, winning professionals rely on visuals. The picture superiority effect is the technical term for the demonstrated fact that humans are significantly better at remembering information when it is presented in visual images, such as logos or characters, rather than in words.

# The Transcender System

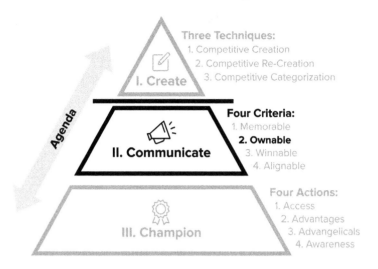

**Three Techniques:**
1. Competitive Creation
2. Competitive Re-Creation
3. Competitive Categorization

I. Create

Agenda

**Four Criteria:**
1. Memorable
**2. Ownable**
3. Winnable
4. Alignable

II. Communicate

**Four Actions:**
1. Access
2. Advantages
3. Advangelicals
4. Awareness

III. Champion

## CHAPTER 9

# Ownable

The best politicians not only create a Campaign Agenda but also *own* it: they believe it, communicate it, act on it, and embrace it. For example, everything about Barack Obama in his 2008 presidential election represented his Agenda of Change. He owned his Agenda by publishing two books that highlighted how his presidency would represent a change in both culture and policies. In 1995, he authored his first book, *Dreams from My Father*, which described the tensions inherent in his mixed racial background. In 2006, three months before announcing his presidential run, he published his best-seller *The Audacity of Hope: Thoughts on Reclaiming the American Dream.* This book highlighted several of Obama's novel—and sometimes controversial—policy ideas, including universal healthcare, which ultimately became known as the Affordable Care Act or "ObamaCare," a policy he signed into law as President on March 23, 2010.

Throughout the 2008 presidential election, Obama communicated, epitomized, and ultimately *owned* his Agenda of Change. On November 4, 2008, Obama was elected the first African American President of the United States.

## CASE STUDY: SWEETGREEN OWNING ITS AGENDA OF "CONNECTING PEOPLE TO REAL FOOD"

The best Transcender companies also *own* their Campaign Agendas. In this example, the healthy-food restaurant chain Sweetgreen is on a mission of "connecting people to real food." I have summarized their Campaign Platform below:

## Sweetgreen Corporate Campaign Platform

| CAMPAIGN AGENDA<br>*"Game" (≤5 words)* | CONNECTING PEOPLE<br>TO REAL FOOD |
|---|---|
| CAMPAIGN C-MESSAGES<br>*Concise communications<br>to push the Campaign<br>Agenda (3 max)* | • Our mission is "to inspire healthier communities by connecting people to real food."<br>• "Democratizing food."<br>• Sweetgreen is a "destination for simple, seasonal, healthy food." |
| CAMPAIGN CANDIDATE<br>*Company or Brand that best<br>fits the Campaign Agenda* | Sweetgreen |
| CANDIDATE POSITIONING<br>*Perception to be created for<br>the Candidate in the minds<br>of stakeholders (≤5 words)* | Simple, Seasonal,<br>Healthy Food |

Transcender companies and professionals are on a *mission*. They are driven by, passionate about—and at times, obsessed with—pushing their Campaign Agenda for a greater good. They believe, and they create believers. As Nathaniel Ru, co-founder and chief brand officer of Sweetgreen, stated in a 2019 *Forbes* article, "In the beginning, we noticed that the food companies with the best marketing were always the unhealthiest. Our thesis was, 'How can we use similar marketing tactics to tell the story of real, healthy food and make it a bigger part of the conversation?' We also realized that simply telling people to eat their vegetables wasn't going to work. We had to connect it to a lifestyle and to our customers' passion points such as music, wellness, and social impact. We looked outside our category to brands like Nike, Supreme, and Patagonia who were leveraging culture and social impact in a way that reinforced their unique point of view. The challenge early on was to change the mindset that we were just a 'salad place' and that Sweetgreen could stand for much more."

Notice the specific words Ru uses: "tell the story," "bigger part of the conversation," "unique point of view," and "change the mindset." This lexicon is very similar to that of a politician; this could easily have been a presidential candidate speaking. Ru knew Sweetgreen had to change the game—from the Traditionalist marketing approach used by "the food companies with the best marketing" to promote unhealthy food—to an election-style campaign with a five-word Agenda: Connecting People to Real Food. Sweetgreen created and communicated this unique Campaign Agenda; their next step was to Champion the Agenda through winning Actions.

Here are the four Actions illustrating how Sweetgreen pursues its Agenda:

**Access** – *Supply Chain*: The key ingredient for Sweetgreen's success is its access to regional and local farmers, which Sweetgreen has carefully vetted and cultivated. In fact, the first Action the company took was to create fast, healthy meals that tasted good and featured ingredients from local farmers. Sweetgreen distinguished itself from other healthy-food, fast-casual food chains by forming direct relationships with its nearby farm-to-table suppliers. According to Ru, "We work with over 150 local farmers across the country to provide the highest quality real food at scale. We have spent countless hours investing in both meaningful relationships with growers but also the technology to serve their products across nearly 100 locations. From seed to store, we are involved in every step of our supply chain which we believe makes for a better-tasting end product."

To further enhance access, Sweetgreen in 2018 initiated its Outpost system: building branded shelving units in offices and apartment buildings to deliver multiple orders directly to customers without lines or fees. The company drops off individual orders at the group delivery locations. This virtual cafeteria concept dramatically increases delivery orders and sales during peak times. "It is part of our initiative to meet customers wherever they are," Sweetgreen CEO Jonathan Neman told *QSR Magazine* about the new initiative. "We're always trying to make it easy and convenient to offer food that is healthy."

**Advantages** – *Technology*: Sweetgreen was one of the first fast-casual chains to offer its own ordering app, design its stores to handle high-volume pickup and delivery orders, and devote extensive space for pickup items, thereby dramatically enhancing order output during the stores' busiest times.

Ru said that "We are always looking for new ways to leverage data and innovation to usher in a future of more easily accessible, real food. As technology advances, we are excited to continue cultivating the relationships that make it all possible, such as breeding new vegetables with innovators like chef Dan Barber and Row 7 and putting ingredients on the blockchain with [IT platform] Ripe.io—all of which allows us to build a more transparent food system, while maximizing flavor profiles."

Sweetgreen is deploying cutting-edge technology to enable customers to trace a salad's ingredients back to the original farm where they were grown. In doing so, the company will literally be Connecting People to Real Food. Ru believes Sweetgreen's "kitchen technology" is already comparable in its technological sophistication to that of Uber.

**Advangelicals/Awareness** – *Sustainability and Community Outreach Programs*: Sweetgreen follows through on its promise to protect the future of real food. Its packaging is derived from 100 percent plant-based, composted materials. The company features the "wastED salad," which is composed of foodstuffs, such as stalks and outer leaves, that result from food prep and are usually thrown away.

In addition, Sweetgreen has initiated community programs to support its mission of "inspiring healthier communities by connecting people to real food." The Sweetgreen in Schools Program teaches local school children the importance of nutrition, fitness, and sustainability. From 2011–2016, Sweetgreen held a popular Sweetlife Festival that offered free concerts, with food proceeds going to its Schools Program. Sweetgreen has partnered with companies like Soul Cycle to host local events with free salads and tasting sessions following cycling classes.

The result of these and other initiatives is devotees who believe in and buy into the company's Agenda of Connecting People to Real Food. According to CNBC, "Now [2019], nearly 12 years in, Sweetgreen has a loyal following of customers who absolutely eat up the brand's ethos: to make 'simple, seasonal, healthy food.'" Over one million patrons have downloaded the Sweetgreen app, which generates most of its food orders.

Sweetgreen has achieved a cult-like status among its passionate patrons. "[Sweetgreen] uses this phrase a lot: 'Democratizing food,' which is so unique in the food space," restaurant consultant Judge Graham told *Eatery*. "They've built almost more of a social, political, cultural brand versus a fast-food occasion." Note that the phrase "Democratizing food" connotes the Transcender concept of "product election" versus the "product selection" approach used by Traditionalist companies.

As of 2020, 13 years after launch, Sweetgreen operates over 90 stores spanning more than eight US states and has revenues exceeding $300 million. The company is valued at more than $1.6 billion and has been called the "Starbucks of Salads." A year earlier, Sweetgreen investor and billionaire Steve Case had remarked to CNBC, "'If I had told you 25 years ago, when Starbucks only had a few locations, that someday it would be a global phenomenon…nobody would have believed that… But that's what happened.' Today, Starbucks has a market value of nearly $90 billion. 'And so that's what we feel with Sweetgreen.'"

In the next chapter, I will discuss how to communicate a *Winning* Campaign Agenda.

## CHAPTER 9 SUMMARY

- The second Agenda criterion is **Ownable**. Like politicians, the best Transcender companies *own* their Campaign Agenda: they believe it, communicate it, act on it, and embrace it.
- The most successful companies and professionals are on a *mission*. They are passionate about pushing their Campaign Agenda for a greater good.
- For example, Sweetgreen owns and demonstrates its Campaign Agenda of Connecting People to Real Food. The company sources natural ingredients from local farmers, offers an easy-to-use ordering app, and is deploying advanced technology to enable customers to trace a salad's ingredients back to its original farm.

# The Transcender System

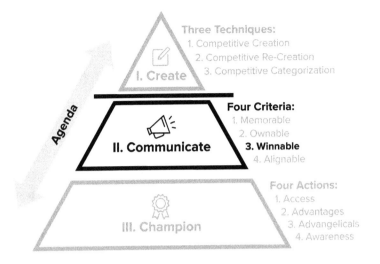

# CHAPTER 10

# Winnable

Traditionalist professionals often ask themselves, "What do my competitors do that keeps me up at night?" In response, I ask them the opposite question: "What can you do to keep *your competitors* up at night?" Transcender leaders shape the market, rather than letting the market shape them. They do so by forcing their will (their Agenda) on the market. They proact rather than react, compelling their competitors to react to them. And, as a result, Transcender leaders are getting *much* better sleep than Traditionalist professionals.

The Traditionalist approach to messaging is to conduct lots of market research, customer focus groups, target segmenting, message testing and re-testing, and so forth. Before the Internet, that often worked. But for data-deluged and over-messaged stakeholders in the Transcender System, that approach doesn't work as well.

For example, in the 2016 presidential election, Hillary Clinton's campaign team suffered from Traditionalist "analysis paralysis"; it extensively researched over 85 different slogans—and never landed on one that worked. While she and her team were testing potential slogans, her rival Donald Trump was repeating, repeating, and repeating Make America Great Again, which was *never* market tested.

Andre Theus, Vice President of Marketing at ProductPlan, clearly expressed this principle in his article "From Brexit to Bernie: What Product Managers Can Learn from Politics":

> Love him or hate him…Trump violated almost every major political rule ever articulated by a campaign manager, Washington pundit, or other expert. And he won! Of all of the rules he broke, perhaps the most important, the one that played the greatest role in his success, was Trump's refusal to ask permission, to listen to what that day's polls said, to change his message for different audiences…

> Similarly, with your products, it is easy to fall into the trap of only soliciting advice from your user and buyer personas, surveying prospects, reading industry analyst reports—and using all this data to develop products you think people will want… You are a leader. You should also know your personas, your market, and the problem that your product solves so well that you'll be in a better

position than even your own customers to know what should comprise your next release.

So how do Transcender companies come up with a winning Campaign Agenda? Transcenders create their Campaign Agenda using one of the three techniques I described in Step I, and then *tell* the market their Campaign Agenda. They still leverage market research, customer insights, and competitive intelligence. However, they do not test a Campaign Agenda using conventional message testing. Trump's Make America Great Again would likely have failed traditional message testing before his presidential campaign communications began. Most voters would have scoffed at such a lofty message emanating from a real estate developer and reality television show host.

*Do not ask the market; tell the market what to think, how to behave, and what to do.* As former President Abraham Lincoln once said, "The best way to predict your future is to create it." Transcender leaders ensure their futures by *creating* the curve, rather than trying to stay ahead of the curve. They are out-of-the-box thinkers and doers who are willing to be different.

## CASE STUDY: HOW NIKE WON WITH ITS "JUST DO IT" CAMPAIGN AGENDA

The classic example of this approach was Nike's "Just Do It" Campaign Agenda. In 1987, Nike was under tremendous competitive pressure from Reebok in the athletic footwear market. Nike reported in 1987 that corporate sales had dropped 18 percent and earnings had declined 40 percent. After explosive growth in the 1970s and early 1980s, Nike was by 1987 losing significant market share to Reebok, which became one of the biggest brand-name phenomena of the decade. Nike desperately needed to change the brand game and effectively relaunch the company. It started with three words: "Just Do It."

In 1987, Dan Wieden, President of Wieden+Kennedy advertising agency, was asked to lead the development of Nike's first major television campaign. In articles in *Dezeen* and *Creative Review*, Wieden explained:

> It was the first television campaign we'd done with some money behind it, so we actually came up with five different 30-second spots. The night before I got a little concerned because there were five different teams working, so there was not an overlying sensibility to them all. Each spot was developed by a different creative team and was markedly different from the others... I felt we needed a tagline to give some unity to the work, one that spoke to the hardest hardcore athletes as well as those taking up a morning walk. So I stayed up that night before and I think I wrote about four or five ideas. I narrowed it down to the last one, which was 'Just Do It.'

> Creatives in the agency all questioned if we really needed it," said Wieden. "Nike questioned it. I said, 'Look, I think we do. I believe we have too many disparate commercials that do not add up to anything without a tagline. I am not married to the thing. We can drop it next round.' A lot of shrugged shoulders, but they let it ride.

To Wieden's credit, he recognized the need for a single, overarching Campaign Agenda that tied together numerous different commercials and messages. Nike recognized the need to go beyond the usual target audience of professional and amateur athletes to anyone even "taking up a morning walk." Nike used Competitive Categorization to create a new activity space: anyone can work out or "Just Do It." In fact, one of the first ads in 1988 for Just Do It showcased Walt Stack, an 80-year-old marathon runner in San Francisco.

Nike was not simply asking customers to buy an athletic shoe or shirt; they were encouraging them to believe in a bold new state of mind. Nike featured the Just Do It campaign through multiple media outlets, including ads, billboards, print media, graffiti art, and merchandise.

The customer response to the Just Do It campaign was overwhelmingly positive. Nike was inundated with phone calls, letters, and—most importantly—sales. During the 10-year period from 1988 to 1998, the campaign helped catapult Nike in its North America sport-shoe business from 18 percent to 43 percent market share, and from $877 million to $9.2 billion in worldwide sales. Nike totally changed the sports-shoe game, ran past pacesetting Reebok, and never looked back.

Following the release of the Just Do It Campaign in 1988, Alice Ruth, a financial analyst for Montgomery Securities, said, "Nike is hitting on all cylinders. They lead the race in terms of consumer demand and retailers' confidence… There is one buzzword among retailers now, and that's Nike." Transcender campaigns create buzz by focusing the attention on their company and products. In the process, they gain market momentum and steal both buzz and share from competitors. In stark contrast, Reebok's advertising at the time was criticized for its lack of focus and clarity. "[Reebok's] advertising message has not been nearly as consistent" as Nike's, said Dusty Kidd, editor of *Sportstyle*, a trade journal.

Importantly, the campaign also revitalized and motivated Nike's own employees. Jerome Conlon, president of Brand Frameworks and a former marketing executive at Nike and Starbucks, said, "Campaigns such as 'Just Do It' are not easy to achieve, but absolutely worth striving for. They have certain uplifting and inspiring qualities that can also energize the internal culture of a company." He wrote in 2015 that Just Do It represented a major turning point. "After the launch of 'Just Do It,' Nike brand sales were rejuvenated, increasing 1,000% over the next ten years."

*Campaign Magazine* described Just Do It as "arguably the best tagline of the 20th century," saying it "cut across age and class barriers, linked Nike with success—and made consumers believe they could be successful too just by wearing its products. For some reason that line resonated deeply in the athletic community and just as deeply with people who had little or no connection to sports… Like all great taglines, it was both simple and memorable. It also suggested something more than its literal meaning, allowing people to interpret it as they wished."

Shortly after Apple's launch of the successful Think Different campaign in 1997, CEO Steve Jobs paid homage to Nike's campaign: "Everyone on the planet can tell you what and who "Just Do It!" stands for. Nike has The Message. It is about athletics and success. Not about shoes. We remember that."

Nike continues to use the tagline across much of its advertising and branding today. "'Just Do It' is still as relevant to us as a brand today as it was 23 years ago," said Davide Grasso, Nike VP of global brand marketing, in 2010. "We actually don't believe in slogans. Instead, what we have found to be most effective is inviting people to join us in what we believe in and what we stand for. And what we stand for is to serve and honor athletes. I think that is why 'Just Do It' has had such an impact over the last 20 years and continues to. It's genuine and speaks to our core mission." Nike wants its customers to *believe* in—not just buy into—its Agenda.

While Traditionalist corporate and agency professionals are constantly changing their brand messages, Transcender professionals create and then communicate a single winning Campaign Agenda, like Just Do It, that stands the test of time. Nike has been using the Just Do It Campaign Agenda for over three decades. Nike is currently the dominant sportswear company in the world, with annual sales exceeding $40 billion, 35 percent more than its nearest rival, Adidas.

So how do Transcender companies know they have a *winning* Agenda, especially since many do not conduct market research to test their Agenda in advance? Here are my seven criteria for determining a winning Agenda (in relative chronological order):

- Does the Agenda resonate with, energize, and rally the company's employees?
- Does the Agenda create tremendous buzz, including many mentions in the media and among industry pundits, and other key market influencers?
- Does the Agenda create a movement of Advangelicals who help espouse the Agenda to others?
- If you Google the company's Agenda with the company's or product's brand name, does the search reveal numerous hits?
- Do customers respond by not only buying the company's products but also believing in the company's Agenda?
- Does it force competitors to react with counter-messaging or other actions?
- Does the Agenda dramatically help the company transcend competitors in terms of market share, sales, profits, and other success measures?

Nike's Just Do It Campaign Agenda checks all these boxes. For example, if you Google "Just Do It" and "Nike," you will find 386,000,000 results—an *incredible* number of mentions.

In the next chapter, I will illustrate how Amazon—another iconic Transcender company—does everything it can to support and align with its stated Campaign Agenda of "Customer Obsession."

## CHAPTER 10 SUMMARY

- ***Do not ask the market; tell the market what to think, how to behave, and what to do.*** Winning leaders force their will (their Agenda) on the market. And they compel their competitors to *react* to them.
- Transcender leaders are not subservient to market research data. They are out-of-the-box thinkers and doers who are willing to be provocative. They create the curve rather than try to stay ahead of it.
- Nike changed the game in 1988 with its "Just Do It" Campaign Agenda, which tied together numerous different commercials and messages. Nike has consistently communicated this same Agenda for over three decades. This winning three-word phrase and its game-changing products have propelled Nike to become the best-selling sportswear company in the world.
- There are seven criteria for a winning Campaign Agenda: energizing employees, customers, and other stakeholders; creating buzz and numerous mentions in the media and by pundits and other influencers; building an Advangelical movement; driving numerous search engine mentions of the Agenda; inspiring customers to believe in the company's products as well as to buy them; forcing competitors to react; and driving up market share and product sales.

# The Transcender System

**Three Techniques:**
1. Competitive Creation
2. Competitive Re-Creation
3. Competitive Categorization

I. Create

**Four Criteria:**
1. Memorable
2. Ownable
3. Winnable
**4. Alignable**

II. Communicate

**Four Actions:**
1. Access
2. Advantages
3. Advangelicals
4. Awareness

III. Champion

Agenda

## CHAPTER 11

# Alignable

The fourth way to communicate a Campaign Agenda is to *align everything a company says and does with the Agenda.* Since the key to winning is Creating the Agenda, then it is essential that all communications, strategies, actions, activities, and measures align with and support the Campaign Agenda.

## CASE STUDY: HOW AMAZON ALIGNS EVERYTHING TO ITS AGENDA

In 1994, Jeff Bezos founded Amazon. Initially, it was an online bookstore with the vision "to be the Earth's most customer-centric company, where customers can find and discover anything they might want to buy online, and endeavors to offer its customers the lowest possible prices." Amazon from the start offered unprecedented access to purchase books from the world's largest virtual storehouse.

As Bezos said, "There are millions of books active in print around the world. The largest physical book superstores only carry about 100,000-150,000 books. So, on the web you could build something that solved a real problem. People cannot find some of these books that they want to find... We basically built Amazon to help people find those hard-to-find books."

Early on, his investors criticized Bezos for allowing negative book reviews to remain on the product pages. They had a Traditionalist mindset: why in the world would any company have anything but positive messages about its products on its own website? They were worried that these unflattering reviews would hurt sales. Bezos responded by stating that Amazon was not in the book business to make sales; it was in the business to help customers get the information they need to make the best purchasing decisions.

Bezos was not playing the Traditionalist brick-and-mortar retail or online retail brand game at Amazon. Bezos created his own game: "Customer Obsession." He was playing a game only Amazon could win.

Bezos' publicly referenced Amazon's Campaign Agenda of Customer Obsession in his 1997 Shareholder Letter:

**Obsess Over Customers:** From the beginning, our focus has been on offering our customers compelling value... We set out to offer customers something they simply could not get any other way and began serving them with books. We brought them much more selection than was possible in a physical store (our store would now occupy 6 football fields), and presented it in a useful, easy-to-search, and easy-to-browse format in a store open 365 days a year, 24 hours a day. We maintained a dogged focus on improving the shopping experience, and in 1997 substantially enhanced our store. We now offer customers gift certificates, 1-Click™ shopping, and vastly more reviews, content, browsing options, and recommendation features. We dramatically lowered prices, further increasing customer value.

Bezos was obsessed from the beginning with providing customers unique and easy access to books. Even with Amazon's expansion into myriad other product lines, here is how Amazon continues to provide customers access to their books today:

- *Universal Book Access*: Most book titles online (nearly 50 million books and counting)
- *Reviews Access*: Critic and user reviews
- *Format Access*: Hardcover, paperback, e-book (via Kindle), and audiobook
- *Value Access*: Multiple price points for different formats
- *Simplicity Access*: "1-Click" ordering; ordering via Alexa device
- *Delivery Access*: Amazon Prime program (same, one- or two-day free delivery), instantaneous Kindle app downloads, third-party delivery
- *Returns Access*: Access to easy returns

According to a 2019 *Vox* article by Jason Del Rey, in the fall of 2004, Amazon was predominantly selling books and videos and was about half the size of eBay, its online sales rival at that time. Amazon was offering "Super Saver Shipping," which required a $25 minimum purchase and promised delivery in 8-10 business days.

The original Amazon Prime program emanated from Bezos' total obsession with customers. In October 2004, Bezos asked his team, "It looks like Super Saver Shipping is working really well for us. Can you bring me some similar ideas for faster shipping?" That question led to a secret project within Amazon, code-named "Futurama." Bezos summoned his team to his boathouse for an urgent Saturday morning meeting to discuss the project status. "'I want to draw a moat around our best customers. I'm going to change the psychology of people not looking at the pennies differences between buying on Amazon versus buying somewhere else,'" Bezos said, according to Vijay Ravindran, Amazon's Director of Ordering at the time. Ravindran added, "And I think that completely changed the mentality. It was brilliant. It made Amazon the default."

At the company's fourth-quarter earnings meeting in 2005, Bezos announced "Amazon Prime," an all-you-can-ship, $79 annual subscription program for one- and two-day free package deliveries. While the company initially lost money on the program, it was a huge hit with customers: Prime members spent seven times more on Amazon products than non-Prime members. Fifteen years later, Bezos announced during the company's fourth-quarter 2020 earnings call that Amazon Prime had surpassed 150 million members across 18 countries. The day after that announcement, the company exceeded a market valuation of $1 trillion for the first time, and became only the fourth company in history to reach that mark.

During those 15 years, Amazon has substantially expanded the Prime Program to offer access to free same-day delivery in selected locations; Prime Video, including Amazon-produced original movies and shows; Amazon Music, with over two million songs; Twitch Prime video games; and Prime Now, offering home delivery for groceries (from Amazon Fresh and Whole Foods Market), pharmacies, and pet stores in two hours or less in over 50 cities globally.

Journalist Del Ray called Amazon Prime "the internet's most successful and devastating membership program" and proclaimed that with Amazon Prime, "Amazon single-handedly—and permanently—raised the bar for convenience in online shopping."

Establishing Amazon Prime was truly a transcendent, game-changing move that demonstrated Amazon's leadership and, as usual, forced competitors to *react* and ultimately play Amazon's Customer Obsession game—a game only Amazon could win. The company has announced plans for its next power play and iteration of Amazon Prime: Amazon Prime Air Delivery Drone.

Here is my summary of Amazon's Campaign Platform:

# Amazon Corporate Campaign Platform

| | |
|---|---|
| **CAMPAIGN AGENDA**<br>*"Game" (≤5 words)* | **CUSTOMER OBESSESION** |
| **CAMPAIGN C-MESSAGES**<br>*Concise communications to push the Campaign Agenda (3 max)* | • "The No. 1 thing that has made us successful by far is obsessive compulsive focus on the customer."<br>• "We see our customers as invited guests to a party, and we are the hosts. It's our job every day to make every important aspect of the customer experience a little bit better."<br>• "Our mission is to be earth's most customer-centric company." |
| **CAMPAIGN CANDIDATE**<br>*Company or Brand that best fits the Campaign Agenda* | **Amazon** |
| **CANDIDATE POSITIONING**<br>*Perception to be created for the Candidate in the minds of stakeholders (≤5 words)* | **Earth's Most Customer-Centric Company** |
| **COMPETITIVE MEASURE(S)** | 80% "Customer Engagement" Metrics |
| **COMPETITOR COUNTER-POSITIONING**<br>*Perception to be created for rivals in the minds of key stakeholders (<5 words)* | *Competitors: Not as Customer Obsessed* |

Interestingly, Amazon does not typically communicate this Campaign Agenda publicly, other than by Bezos in shareholder communications or business-to-business type interviews. Like Starbucks, Amazon *implicitly* demonstrates its Agenda to its customers.

Amazon's Campaign Agenda, Positioning, and measures all incorporate the word "customer": *Customer* Obsession, *Customer*-Centric, and *Customer* Engagement. When the Product Positioning and the Competitive Measures echo the same words as the Campaign Agenda, it is called "Triple Alignment," a powerful way to support and win with a Campaign Agenda. Triple Alignment helps to ensure that all communications and actions align with the Campaign Agenda. For instance, notice how one German-based Amazon executive, Florian Baumgartner, Director Consumables, describes Agenda alignment at the company: "Amazon is a company driven by a relentless customer focus. We believe that customers always want something better, and it is our desire to delight them. This drives us to invent on their behalf. At Amazon, all of our actions, goals, projects, programs, and inventions begin and end with the customer in mind."

Note that Bezos leads with the Agenda of Customer Obsession when he talks, and follows that with the company's Positioning as the "Earth's Most Customer-Centric Company." Bezos not only talks the talk; he walks the walk. Everything Amazon does focuses on customers. For example, on the Amazon Jobs website page, the #1 Amazon "Leadership Principle" is Customer Obsession: *"Leaders start with the customer and work backwards. They work vigorously to earn and keep customer trust. Although leaders pay attention to competitors, they obsess over customers."*

To ensure that all his employees and partners are aligned with the company's Agenda of Customer Obsession, Bezos uses a performance measurement system in which 80 percent of the metrics are based on "Customer Engagement." For example, Amazon has established customer engagement metrics for the professional selling partners on its website to ensure they meet or exceed Amazon's high expectations for its customers. Amazon rates its selling partners on a variety of customer engagement metrics, including Order Defect Rate ("ODR"), Buyer-Seller Ratings, and Late Shipment Rates. Any customer order that has negative seller feedback (e.g., poor product delivery condition, negative feedback rate, credit card chargeback) is considered a "defect" by Amazon and is calculated into a seller's ODR rating. Amazon has set a high bar of <1 percent failure for the ODR metric. Amazon uses overall seller ratings to select or exclude selling partners.

Amazon executed on Bezos' Customer Obsession Agenda so effectively across numerous types of products that the company passed rival Walmart in 2015 to become the world's most valuable retailer. The following year, Bezos reaffirmed Amazon's passion for pleasing its customers and repeated his Campaign Agenda of "Customer Obsession" in his 2016 Amazon Shareholders' Letter:

> **True Customer Obsession:** There are many ways to center a business. You can be competitor focused, you can be product focused, you can be technology focused, you can be business model focused, and there are more. But in my view, obsessive customer focus is by far the most important. Why? There are many advantages to a customer-centric approach, but here is the big one: customers are always beautifully, wonderfully dissatisfied, even when they report being happy and business is great. Even when they do not

yet know it, customers want something better, and your desire to delight customers will drive you to invention on their behalf... A customer-obsessed culture best creates the conditions where all of that can happen.

Stephen Bavister, a LexisClick marketing consultant who has written extensively on customer obsession, said, "We've been researching 'Customer Obsession' extensively over the last 12 months. There is one organization that comes up time and time again and it is Amazon. Amazon's success can be attributed to a number of factors; however, Jeff Bezos gives the top spot to Customer Obsession." In 2019, more than 20 years after founding Amazon, Bezos asserted, "The No. 1 thing that has made us successful by far is obsessive compulsive focus on the customer."

## CHAPTER 11 SUMMARY

- Amazon's CEO Jeff Bezos did not play the Traditionalist retail or online retail brand game at Amazon. Bezos created his own game: "Customer Obsession." He was playing a game only Amazon could win.
- *Everything must align with the Agenda.* The fourth way to communicate a Campaign Agenda is to align everything a company says and does with the Agenda. For example, virtually everything Amazon does aligns with its Customer Obsession Agenda; all its communications, strategies, actions, activities, and metrics focus on customers.
- This focus aligns Amazon's employees and its partners to create the "Earth's most customer-centric company," which is the corporate positioning. For example, Amazon's #1 Leadership Principle for its employees is "Customer Obsession";

most of its demanding performance metrics for its partners are customer focused.

- Amazon Prime was truly a transcendent, game-changing move that demonstrated Amazon's leadership and compelled competitors to *react* and ultimately play Amazon's Customer Obsession game.

# CHAMPION
# THE AGENDA

# The Transcender System

## CHAPTER 12

# Access

Traditionalist marketers are aware of the "4 P's" of the so-called "Marketing Mix:" product (the good or service), price (what the consumer pays), place (location where a product is marketed), and promotion (marketing tactics). This idea originated in the 1940s and was later formalized by E. Jerome McCarthy in his 1960 book *Basic Marketing: A Managerial Approach.* This Traditionalist toolkit has been the foundation for marketing planning for over 60 years.

The Internet has forced an overhaul to this conventional

approach. In the Transcender System, I have identified the 4 A's, or Actions, which align with and support the Campaign Platform: *Access, Advantages, Advangelicals, and Awareness.* I will discuss each of these "A's" in turn over the next four chapters, starting with *Access.*

There are two types of Transcender System Access: *Limited* and *Unlimited.* For example, the Internet created virtually *unlimited* access not only to information but also to myriad other products, services, offerings, and technologies, such as:

- *Books*: Amazon
- *Music*: Apple iTunes
- *Vacation Homes*: Airbnb Rentals
- *Ridesharing Services*: Uber, Lyft
- *Movies/TV Shows*: Netflix

The Internet made books and innumerable other goods and services accessible, available, and affordable. Access to these products is typically offered for a relatively small fee, which provides high value. In the Traditionalist System, pricing was a huge factor and one of the traditional 4 P's. However, in the Transcender System, *Access* provides multifaceted value and has therefore become significantly more important than price.

For instance, when customers buy a relatively expensive espresso at Starbucks, they are not simply paying for a cup of coffee. They are getting *access* to significantly more value: a convenient place to sit and prepare for work or to decompress after work; a relaxed environment in which to meet friends; a comfortable "family room" with cozy couches, free Wi-Fi, and pleasant music; and clean restroom facilities.

Similarly, millions of people have been willing to pay a relatively high price of $500 to $1,000 for Apple's iPhones because of their perceived value beyond that of a simple mobile phone. The hundreds of thousands of applications that the iPhone offers provide almost unlimited value.

Because of the Internet, saving time and avoiding hassle have become increasingly important parts of the value equation. There is a small but significant group of cycle enthusiasts who are willing to pay $2,500 for Peloton's home exercise bike because of its additional value to them, in terms of home access, professional-quality cycling equipment, privacy, and time savings from eliminating the drive to a cycling studio. Peloton users also pay additional monthly fees for remote access to thousands of live and recorded group classes, the competitive "Peloton Leaderboard," and personal cycling metrics.

Internet-based subscription payment models enable consumers to get access both to more products (e.g., Apple downloaded music, Netflix streaming movies) and to higher-end offerings (e.g., Airbnb vacation homes, Rent the Runway designer apparel), albeit for a *limited* amount of time.

## CASE STUDY: HOW GOOGLE PROVIDES FREE ACCESS TO THE WORLD'S INFORMATION

When I think of leveraging Access to win, the company that comes immediately to mind is Google. No company on the planet has focused more on providing access to the world's information. According to David A. Vise, author of *The Google Story*:

Not since Gutenberg invented the modern printing press more than 500 years ago, making books and scientific tomes affordable and widely available to the masses, has any new invention empowered individuals, and transformed access to information, as profoundly as Google. With its colorful, childlike logo set against a background of pure white, Google's magical ability to produce speedy, relevant responses to queries hundreds of millions of times daily has changed the way people find information.

Ironically, Google's founders initially did not even plan to start a company. In the late 1990s, two Stanford University graduate students, Sergey Brin and Larry Page, were unhappy with the quality of existing search engines. To please themselves, they teamed up to find a better way to organize and access all the information on the Internet. Page found a methodology to prioritize search results by ranking a website's links instead of merely counting them; he fittingly called his approach "PageRank." Using this novel technique and others, the two created a dramatically more powerful and accurate search engine.

In 1998, they founded Google with the mission: "To organize the world's information and make it universally accessible and useful." Initially, they focused on enhancing access to online information by improving their search engine technology. By 2007, Google launched "Universal Search," which accessed multiple types of searched sources, including websites, and eventually news, images, videos, shopping, maps, finance, arts, culture, and more.

However, an *offline* Google initiative demonstrated the length to which the founders would go to provide free access to the world's information. Brin and Page wanted to scan books from large and prestigious libraries around the world, including the

University of Michigan, Stanford, Oxford, Harvard, and the New York Public Library. Digitizing these books would provide their users with computer access to not just popular works but also to rare and ancient published works from distant libraries.

Announcing the book collaboration, Mary Jo Coleman, the University of Michigan's president, stated, "The University of Michigan's partnership with Google offers three overarching qualities that help fulfill our mission: the preservation of books; worldwide access to information; and, most importantly, the public good of the diffusion of knowledge." In making her announcement, Coleman called the Google library project the "most revolutionary enterprise she has experienced."

In fact, Google offers unparalleled access to the world's largest online repository of human knowledge. Transcenders create *revolutionary*, not evolutionary, offerings. This project reflected Larry Page's personal mantra of a "healthy disregard for the impossible"—a common theme for Transcenders who set and often achieve lofty goals.

Google by then had become profitable by including small stamp-size ads to the right of, and clearly separated from, their carefully generated search results. As a result, it was able to invest about $400 million to speed up the process of digitizing books. The company scanned over 25 million books from around the world. While copyright and other intellectual property concerns limit full access to certain books, the company offers a range of access levels, from full access to snippets.

This initiative and other actions demonstrate that Google does not act like a Traditionalist company. For example, unlike its rival Yahoo, Google has never sold ads on its home page, arguably the most valuable virtual real estate on the web. The company makes money by selling ads but strives to ensure they are relevant to users.

According to Vise, "Google does not try to make as much money as it could in the short run… Google displays no advertising on its [homepage], forgoing hundreds of millions of dollars in revenue and profits, to give users a high-quality search experience." Google knows that adding ads would slow the delivery of search results to its users. Google is seeking to provide a *transcendent experience* for its customers. Vise added that Google has "a laser-like focus on serving the best interests of Google users. They, in turn, become its best advocates." Google has democratized the web's information. The company consistently and relentlessly seeks to uphold its mission of rapidly providing universal search information that is free and accessible to everyone.

Here is my summary of Google's Campaign Platform:

## Google Corporate Campaign Platform

| CAMPAIGN AGENDA<br>*"Game"* (≤5 words) | ACCESS TO THE<br>WORLD'S INFORMATION |
|---|---|
| ***CAMPAIGN C-MESSAGES***<br>*Concise communications*<br>*to push the Campaign*<br>*Agenda* (<u>3</u> max) | • Google's mission is "to organize the world's information and make it universally accessible and useful."<br>• "That's why Search makes it easy to discover a broad range of information from a wide variety of sources."<br>• Google provides "unbiased, accurate and free access to information for those who rely on us around the world." |
| ***CAMPAIGN CANDIDATE***<br>*Company or Brand that best*<br>*fits the Campaign Agenda* | **Google** |
| ***CANDIDATE POSITIONING***<br>*Perception to be created for*<br>*the Candidate in the minds*<br>*of stakeholders* (≤5 words) | **Universal, Free<br>Information Access** |

In their first Shareholder Letter in 2004, the company's founders stated that "Google is not a conventional company. We do not intend to become one. Throughout Google's evolution as a privately held company, we have managed Google differently. We...provide unbiased, accurate and free access to information for those who rely on us around the world." Google never has been a Traditionalist company; they have always charted their own course and played their own very successful game.

## CASE STUDY: ZARA'S UNLIMITED AND LIMITED ACCESS TO FAST FASHION

Some Transcender companies offer both unlimited *and* limited access. For example, Zara is a Spain-based apparel retailer that targets primarily young, fashion- and price-conscious adults. A market analysis by UK Essays found that "Zara releases around 10,000 different designs every year and deliberately produces styles in small quantities to create an aura of scarcity. This ensures that customers visit regularly to see the latest designs and purchase immediately because there is no certainty that the style will be there the next day."

Social psychologists refer to this approach as the scarcity principle: something high in demand but low in supply is seen as more valuable. Masoud Golsorkhi, editor of the UK-based fashion magazine *TANK*, observed, "When you went to Gucci or Chanel in October, you knew the chances were good that clothes would still be there in February. With Zara, you know that if you do not buy it, right then and there, within 11 days the entire stock will change. You buy it now or never. And because the prices are so low, you buy it now."

Starting in the late 1990s, several retailers pioneered "Fast Fashion": producing and marketing fashion clothing collections based on the latest runway and fashion trends. However, it was Zara that changed and ultimately owned the so-called "Fast Fashion" game. In 2008, Louis Vuitton's Fashion Director Daniel Piette described Zara as "possibly the most innovative retailer in the world."

Founded in 1975 and based in Galicia, Spain, the company's mission is to provide fast and affordable fashionable items. In Transcender terms, the company's two-word Campaign Agenda could be "Fast Fashion"; in fact, the Zara name has become almost synonymous with the term.

The retailer became the world's largest clothing retailer primarily by leveraging product access. Here are the 4 A's of Zara's Transcender approach:

*Advantages*: Zara's main competitive advantage is its superior supply chain: Zara can introduce and distribute new designs to its stores within two weeks of a new style appearing on fashion runways, a feat unmatched by its competitors. Zara vertically and horizontally integrated its global operations; it handles product design, production, and distribution in-house in Spain. This has enabled Zara to launch as many as 10,000 clothing items annually, compared to 2,000-4,000 for its rivals H&M and Gap. Moreover, Zara has dramatically reduced time to market and inventory levels. Zara's typical store keeps only six days of inventory, as opposed to 52 days for H&M.

*Access*: In addition to offering thousands of different clothing items a year, Zara also offers ready access to its over 2,000 stores in 93 countries, each of which is strategically located near its targeted customers. The company also operates across 39 online markets, which are linked with store merchandise. For example, customer store visits are linked online to offer additional access to inventory not present in a specific location.

Zara uses technology, including augmented reality, to enhance the customer retail experience. Using their cellphones, shoppers can visualize models showcasing selected clothing items by clicking on store sensors or augmented-reality-enabled shop windows. According to retail expert Shelley E. Kohan of the Fashion Institute of Technology, "The more quickly and efficiently a customer can navigate through the store to explore and find hidden gems, the better the experience. Zara nails that."

She further explained in a 2018 *Forbes* article, "While Zara is an excellent purveyor of product, it also capitalizes on the store experience by continuously offering reasons for customers to visit the stores and catch the hottest trends at affordable prices." Zara has cultivated loyal customers who typically visit its stores 17 times per year, four times the rate of rival retailers.

*Advangelicals/Awareness*: Because of these meaningful interactions, many Zara customers become Advangelicals who spread the word about the latest fashion offerings and improve the company's products. Zara has over 30 million followers on Instagram, approximately 14 million on Twitter, and 1.8 million on WeChat, China's largest social media app.

In 2016, Kohan found that Zara customer service representatives replied to more than 17 million customer inquiries. She says, "Zara actually listens and reacts to customer feedback as its most valuable brand asset to improve its products and services... The result is the customer and the company work cooperatively together so that the Zara customer becomes the *Chief Customer Officer*, providing feedback on all aspects of the business." By carefully cultivating close customer relationships, Zara gains real-time feedback to expedite and enhance the company's operations. This represents another means by which the company fulfills its industry-leading Campaign Agenda of Fast Fashion.

In the next chapter, I will discuss how Tesla leverages the second "A", *Advantages*, to lead the global electric car market.

# CHAPTER 12 SUMMARY

- Traditionalist marketers use the 4 P's of marketing: Product, Price, Place, and Promotion. In contrast, Transcenders leverage the "4 A's," or Actions, to support the Campaign Platform: *Access*, *Advantages*, *Advangelicals*, and *Awareness*.

- *Win by offering limited and unlimited product access.* The Internet created virtually unlimited access not only to information but also to myriad other products, services, offerings, and technologies.

- Google became the leading online search engine by offering unlimited, free access to the world's information. In contrast, Zara became the world's largest fast-fashion retailer by leveraging Internet-based information to offer speedy access to clothing apparel, but typically only for a short period of time.

# The Transcender System

Three Techniques:
1. Competitive Creation
2. Competitive Re-Creation
3. Competitive Categorization

I. Create

Four Criteria:
1. Memorable
2. Ownable
3. Winnable
4. Alignable

II. Communicate

Four Actions:
1. Access
**2. Advantages**
3. Advangelicals
4. Awareness

III. Champion

Agenda

CHAPTER 13

# Advantages

Leading Transcender companies combine winning campaigns with winning products that may offer multiple competitive advantages. Tesla best exemplifies the second "A" in the Transcender System: *Advantages*. Engineers Martin Eberhard and Marc Tarpenning founded Tesla Motors, Inc. in 2003. They named the company after the inventor and electrical engineer Nikola Tesla, who helped develop modern alternating current (AC), the form in which electric power is delivered to consumers.

Elon Musk joined the company's board of directors in 2004 as chairman and major Tesla investor. He envisioned Tesla as a technology company and independent automaker with the goal of offering affordable electric cars to everyone. Musk took an active product role at Tesla, helping develop its first car, the all-electric Roadster, which was launched in 2008.

Musk became Tesla's CEO and Product Architect in 2008. He stated in 2013, "Our goal when we created Tesla a decade ago was the same as it is today: to accelerate the advent of sustainable transport by bringing compelling mass-market electric cars to market as soon as possible." Three years later, Musk revised the corporate mission as their Agenda grew: "to accelerate the world's transition to sustainable **encrgy**" to reflect the company's forays in battery storage and solar energy as well.

Here is my summary of Tesla's Campaign Platform:

## Tesla Corporate Campaign Platform

| | |
|---|---|
| **CAMPAIGN AGENDA**<br>*"Game"* (≤5 words) | **WORLD'S TRANSITION<br>TO SUSTAINABLE ENERGY** |
| **CAMPAIGN C-MESSAGES**<br>*Concise communications<br>to push the Campaign<br>Agenda (3 max)* | • "In order to have clean air in cities, you have to go electric."<br>• "Tesla is here to stay and keep fighting for the electric car revolution."<br>• "We will not stop until every car on the road is electric." |
| **CAMPAIGN CANDIDATE**<br>*Company or Brand that best<br>fits the Campaign Agenda* | **Tesla** |
| **CANDIDATE POSITIONING**<br>*Perception to be created for<br>the Candidate in the minds<br>of stakeholders (≤5 words)* | **Compelling Mass-<br>Market Electric Cars** |

## CASE STUDY: TESLA'S ADVANTAGES

Musk stated, "When somebody has a breakthrough innovation, it is rarely one little thing. Very rarely, is it one little thing. It's usually a whole bunch of things that collectively amount to a huge innovation." I chose Tesla to demonstrate winning Advantages because the company re-created the automobile literally from the battery up, since Tesla designed and built its vehicles around its unique lithium-ion batteries. This enabled the company to reimagine cars in ways that Traditionalist car manufacturers could not, because they in effect were trying to retrofit their existing combustion engine cars to be electrically powered.

I call these Tesla's "S" Advantages because the plurality emphasizes the *multiple* Advantages that Tesla offers with its electric vehicles:

- *Savings:* True to its Campaign Agenda, Tesla's electric cars dramatically save gas and reduce carbon emissions compared to internal-combustion engine cars. To offer a compelling mass-market car, Tesla initially priced the Model 3 sedan at $35,000. By 2021, the starting price had increased to $38,990, still a 30 percent savings compared to the average cost of other US electric vehicles.

In countries around the world, Tesla owners have also benefited from various types of government incentives to purchase plug-in electric cars, such as purchase rebates, tax exemptions, and tax credits.

In addition, Tesla currently offers Tesla owners in California automobile insurance at rates that are up to 20 percent (and in certain cases, up to 30 percent) lower than those offered by traditional auto insurance companies. Tesla can offer these savings to its drivers because its advanced technology captures extensive car data, including maintenance and service records. Tesla also eliminates the standard auto insurance fees. The company intends to expand its insurance operation to additional US states in the future.

- *Sales model:* In contrast to conventional auto manufacturers' dealer networks, Tesla primarily sells its vehicles online. This distinctive approach enables customers to customize, order, and purchase their vehicles online without ever seeing or test driving the cars. Additionally, Tesla maintains a limited number of stores and "galleries"—some based in malls—to showcase its models.

- *Stations*: Tesla has built its own global network of super-charging stations, battery swap stations, and service stations.
- *Software*: The company regularly updates its automotive software, often overnight, so that some customers feel like they are almost getting a new vehicle.
- *Service*: Tesla cars require minimal maintenance compared to gas-powered cars. For example, the company only recommends brake replacements annually (for cars in cold-weather regions) and air conditioning services every few years.
- *Speed*: Tesla's cars have incredible acceleration rates. Tesla claims that its Model S "Plaid" sedan has the quickest acceleration on earth for a production car: from zero to 60 mph in less than *two* seconds. Musk once stated that the Tesla "will crush a Porsche on the track, just crush it. If you like fast cars, you'll love this car."
- *Safety*: Tesla models typically receive high safety ratings. In 2018, the National Highway Traffic Safety Administration awarded the Tesla Model S the best safety rating of any car ever tested and the highest safety rating overall, with a combined Vehicle Safety Score (provided to manufacturers) of 5.4 stars out of 5. Of all vehicles tested, including every major make, model, and vehicle type approved for sale in the United States, the 2018 Model S set a record for the lowest likelihood of injury to occupants.
- *Single Charge Range*: In 2021, Tesla debuted the Model S Plaid, which can go over 520 miles on a single charge, which is currently the longest range of any mass-market electric vehicle.
- *Self-driving option*: Tesla offered one of the first commercially available partially automated highway driving and self-parking systems in its cars.

Taken together, these advantages reinforce Tesla's Positioning of offering a "compelling mass-market electric car" for which some customers are willing to pay more. Musk says that "there is a lot of potential if you have a compelling product and people are willing to pay a premium for that. I think that is what Apple has shown. You can buy a much cheaper cellphone or laptop, but Apple's product is so much better than the alternative, and people are willing to pay that premium."

Importantly, Traditionalist automobile companies seek competitive advantages, typically one or two relatively minor improvements over competitors' products that they can use to differentiate their brand. For example, Traditional auto manufacturers like Ford, Chevy, and Dodge are constantly trying to differentiate their trucks based on relatively minor enhancements in horsepower, towing capabilities, and payload capacities. In contrast, Transcenders like Tesla create "Transcendent Advantages": multiple, dramatic developments in their products relative to rivals' products.

Tesla demonstrates not only Transcendent Advantages but also the remaining three A's:

**Access:** Tesla's 2016 unveiling of the Model 3 vehicle illustrates how the company utilizes both unlimited and limited access to sell cars. The Model 3 solved the dual challenge of electric cars: typically high cost and low cruising range per charge. At that time, the Model 3 was Tesla's least expensive car (starting at $35,000), yet boasting a category-leading range of 200 miles on a single charge (comparable to Chevrolet's Bolt). This combination of low price and high cruising range provided the mass market with dramatically greater access to an appealing electric car.

However, Tesla offered very limited initial production of the car, creating a first-come, first-served mentality. This use of the scarcity principle, in combination with the Tesla 3's low price and high cruising range, drove demand sky-high. In an April 2016 *Forbes* article entitled "Tesla's Unbelievable Model 3 Pre-Order Mirage: Be Careful What You Wish For," journalist Bertell Schmitt wrote, "When Tesla's Elon Musk took to the stage to reveal the Model 3 on March 31, 2016, he already had 115,000 reservations placed by people who paid $1,000 for the privilege to get in line for a car that might not ship in considerable volume until 2019. [Two weeks later], the number of Model 3 pre-orders stood at 276,000… To put the unbelievable number of pre-orders even more in perspective, the world's best-selling electric vehicle, the Nissan Leaf, had sold a total 211,000 units globally since its launch in 2010 [6 years earlier]."

To enhance the perception of Model 3 scarcity and increase demand, Musk would regularly update the rising reservation numbers via Twitter. The company claimed that demand for the Model 3 exceeded 1,800 orders daily, and that it "was struggling to keep up." By July 2017, Tesla reported over 500,000 reservations. *Bloomberg News* claimed that "the Model 3's unveiling was unique in the 100-year history of the mass-market automobile." Musk fanned the flames in October 2016 by tweeting, "We are deep in production hell"—due in part to actual production issues.

In the third quarter of 2017, Tesla delivered its first 200 Model 3 cars and soon ramped up production. By February 2019, the Model 3 had surpassed the Chevrolet Volt as the all-time best-selling electric car in the United States. By March 2020, Tesla had sold more than 500,000 Model 3 cars, enabling it to surpass the Nissan Leaf to become the world's best-selling electric car.

**Awareness:** By all accounts, Elon Musk is a successful serial entrepreneur and a business icon, having founded or co-founded the companies SpaceX, The Boring Company, Neurolink, and OpenAI. But he is also a brilliant marketer who knows how to create and maintain awareness for Tesla. Musk is the face of the company and acts in the following ways like a politician:

- *Visionary*: Musk seeks to promote climate change by "accelerating the world's transition to sustainable energy."
- *High-Profile*: Musk is constantly tweeting, to the degree that Tesla is regularly one of the top three automakers on social media, despite the company's significantly lower media spending. The charismatic Musk is a *tour de force* on social media, with more than 10,000 tweets and 45 million followers, nine times the number of Tesla corporate followers. He has appeared in multiple television shows and movies, including *The Simpsons*, *South Park*, *The Big Bang Theory*, *Saturday Night Live*, and *Iron Man 2*.
- *Boundary Pushing*: Musk sent a Tesla Model S (with a dummy in the driver's seat) into space orbit aboard one of his SpaceX rockets.

**Advangelicals:** In many ways, Musk himself is the ultimate Tesla Advangelical. He is not only high profile, but also very responsive to customers' social media tweets, sometimes referring product suggestions to his Tesla design teams, and he often updates his followers on Tesla's activities.

A 2019 *Consumer Reports* survey revealed that "Tesla has the highest owner satisfaction rating among all brands by a wide margin." Similarly, a 2019 *Bloomberg* survey of 5,000 Model 3 owners found that 99 percent of respondents would recommend the Model 3 to their family or friends, and 99 percent said that the vehicle had surpassed their expectations and would buy the vehicle again.

A J.D. Power Automotive Survey in 2020 ranked Tesla cars highest among all US automobiles in "appeal," a measurement of owner's emotional attachment and excitement. This is despite the fact the J.D. Power Automotive Quality Survey, conducted the same year, ranked Tesla cars *last* in quality, based on the number of car defects reported annually. Regarding the two surveys, Doug Betts, J.D. Power Automotive Division President, commented, "The people love the car; they appear to accept issues that come along with it. In the end, loyalty will be something to look at, particularly if other companies start to offer some of the same features and things that Tesla has [with fewer defects]—will they be lured away?"

Longtime automotive executive Philippe Chain said, "What would have been deemed as unacceptable by any car maker [*sic*] was seen as part of an ongoing process by Elon Musk who believed, rightly so, that the user experience of driving a truly innovative automobile would outweigh minor defects that will eventually be corrected." Clearly, Tesla owners have bought into Musk's concept of compelling mass-market electric cars with numerous Advantages, and are therefore willing to overlook the cars' many defects.

This approach is a direct contrast to Traditionalist car manufacturers. In 2020, Wharton Business Professor Rahul Kapoor said, "The established automakers have come across as being apprehensive, taking a bit of a backseat... [They] have been taking more piecemeal strategies: 'Let's try this. Let's try this... But...[t]hat thinking has to change. They have to be much more aggressive." In essence, Transcender Tesla has changed the car manufacturing game, and is driving the world's largest automakers to respond with revolutionary rather than evolutionary changes—not their forte. Separately, Kapoor commented that "the key for these automakers will be to try and change the rules of the game that Tesla is playing." Tesla is forcing Traditionalist rivals to play a game only it can win.

Tesla has gained another competitive advantage by generating cult-like Advangelicals who promote the brand, volunteer at Tesla stores, and join Tesla auto clubs. In her November 2019 *Mashable* article, "Why Tesla Inspires Such Devoted Fans," reporter Sasha Lekach showcased several Tesla Advangelicals. She featured Vivianna and Peter Van Deerlin, a couple who initiated a "Tesla Bootcamp," an educational workshop for Tesla owners to learn about their cars, and took their Tesla Model 3 on a 3,180-mile, cross-country road trip—without filling up once on gas. Vivianna explained that "Tesla is more than a car and energy products company; it is a community of owners with many things in common, including a concern for the environment and a love of their Tesla vehicles."

Sasha Lekach explained the rationale powering Tesla's fandom: "Why are Tesla fans so devoted to the brand? It is because *Tesla has transcended a mere car brand.* It has become a community, experience, and way of life. In the same way that Apple changed the concept of a cellphone, Tesla acolytes think the Model S, X, 3, and forthcoming cars like the Model Y and pickup truck, can change not only electric vehicles, but all personally-owned cars."

The advantages of Tesla's cars—combined with unique access, social media awareness, and devoted Advangelicals—have driven Tesla to become the world's best-selling manufacturer of plug-in battery-powered electric cars in the world. In December

2020, Tesla's market value exceeded that of the next nine global automobile manufacturers *combined*. On January 8, 2021, Tesla reached a market capitalization exceeding $800 billion, making it the fifth most valuable company in the world after Apple, Microsoft, Amazon, and Alphabet (Google's parent company).

## CHAPTER 13 SUMMARY

- Transcender companies combine winning campaigns with winning products that may offer multiple competitive advantages. Tesla best exemplifies the second "A" in the Transcender System: *Advantages*.
- Tesla CEO Musk stated, "When somebody has a breakthrough innovation, it is rarely one little thing. Very rarely, is it one little thing. It's usually a **whole bunch of things that collectively amount to a huge innovation**." Musk has ensured that Tesla offers a "whole bunch" of advantages in its cars, compared to those of its rivals.
- Tesla's Campaign Agenda is the "World's Transition to Sustainable Energy" and the company positions its vehicles as "compelling mass-market electric cars." Launched in 2016, Tesla's Model 3 combined low price and long range to provide dramatically greater consumer access to an appealing electric car.
- The advantages of Tesla's cars—combined with unique access, social media awareness, and devoted Advangelicals—have driven Tesla to become the world's best-selling manufacturer of plug-in battery-powered electric cars, with a market valuation that dwarfs other Traditionalist car manufacturers. By leveraging a Transcender approach, Tesla became the fifth most valuable company in the world in 2021.

# The Transcender System

**Three Techniques:**
1. Competitive Creation
2. Competitive Re-Creation
3. Competitive Categorization

I. Create

Agenda

**Four Criteria:**
1. Memorable
2. Ownable
3. Winnable
4. Alignable

II. Communicate

**Four Actions:**
1. Access
2. Advantages
**3. Advangelicals**
4. Awareness

III. Champion

## CHAPTER 14

# Advangelicals

Winning presidential candidates use their Campaign Agendas to inspire others to stand with and work for them. Both Barack Obama and Donald Trump motivated their followers to push for their respective Campaign Agendas of "Change" and "Make America Great Again." Through those movements, they generated avalanches of support that ultimately propelled them into office, where they could execute their Agendas.

Similarly, consistently winning sports teams like the US Women's National Soccer Team and the New Zealand National Rugby

Team recognize the value of igniting momentum—a *movement*—not only within their teams, but also among their fans, to help them win games. "Fans," of course, is short for fanatics. Both politicians and coaches understand the importance of uniting a passionate fan base under a shared cause. The best Transcender professionals do the same.

In my consulting work, I have found that **Traditionalist companies have a mission; Transcender companies are on a mission.** For many Traditionalist companies, a mission statement is often simply a statement they put up on their website, whereas for Transcender companies, it is the guiding principle in everything they do. In 2015, Amazon's CEO Jeff Bezos distinguished between "missionaries" and "mercenaries" in the business world. "The missionary is building the product and building the service because they love the customer, because they love the product, because they love the service. The mercenary is building the product or service so that they can flip the company and make money." He added in 2018, "It's usually the missionaries who make the most money."

Peloton has created what *Elle* magazine recently referred to as the "Peloverse." Dr. Jenna Jacobson, an assistant professor of retail management at Ryerson University, said that "all cult fitness brands have online followings, but Peloton's is more than a fandom: it's a core part of the company's corporate identity, a lifeline for thousands of riders, and, increasingly, the secret sauce that separates Peloton from an exploding field of internet-connected competitors. [Peloton] has really become embedded into individual's lifestyles."

Similarly, Tesla is on a global mission to inspire people to transition to sustainable energy. If people believe in that mission (and can afford a Tesla car), they will buy into the company's Agenda, purchase their electric vehicles, and, importantly, advocate for and inspire others to do so. The most successful Transcender companies transform their Campaign Agenda into a *movement*.

## TO CHANGE THE MARKET, CREATE AN ADVANGELICAL MOVEMENT

Do you believe in Peloton's digital fitness or Tesla's sustainable energy mission? If so, you are more likely to become at least a customer, and, at best, an Advangelical. **Advangelicals** represent the third "A" in the Transcender System, after Access and Advantages. I define Advangelicals as stakeholders who advocate, advise, promote, and inspire others to believe in a company's Campaign Agenda.

In politics, winning is all about changing the narrative. In business, winning is all about changing the game. To change the game and overwhelm your competition, create an Advangelical Movement: an army of Campaign Advangelicals.

Transcender Advangelicals are very different from Traditionalist Advocates, as shown in the comparison chart below:

# Comparison Chart: Traditionalist *Advocates* vs. Transcender *Advangelicals*

| Differences | Traditionalist System *Advocates* | Transcender System *Advangelicals* |
|:---:|:---:|:---:|
| *They Are* | Product Influencers | Passionate Proselytizers |
| *They Support* | The Brand | The Agenda |
| *They Create* | Positive Reviews | Agenda Converts |
| *They Offer* | Product Feedback | Product Suggestions |
| *They Tell* | Their Social Circle: Friends and Family | Their Social Media: Followers and Fans |

Advocates are product influencers who support the brand by writing positive product reviews and occasionally offering product feedback to the company. They primarily tell their social circle—usually friends and family—about the product. In contrast, Advangelicals do all those things, *but much more.* Advangelicals are passionate proselytizers who promote the company's Campaign Agenda, and convert followers to push the Agenda, by leveraging social media. In some cases, they may suggest specific product improvements or new product ideas. Importantly, Advangelicals feel like "part of the family"; they're not just customers—they see themselves as an integral part of the business.

These Advangelical characteristics are illustrated by the following two case studies.

## CASE STUDY: LEMI SHINE CREATES A DISHWASHING ADVANGELICAL MOVEMENT

While it is easy to understand why customers could become Advangelical about sustainable energy, how can companies get customers to be passionate about more mundane issues and products, such as dishwashing detergents? Lemi Shine, a small Texas-based, family-owned manufacturer of household cleaning products, demonstrates how.

This company competes in the highly competitive dishwashing detergent category that is dominated by established big Traditionalist players and products, including Procter & Gamble's *Cascade* and Reckitt Benckiser's *Finish*. There was no way the tiny company could begin to match the huge advertising budgets of its behemoth rivals. Lemi Shine and its marketing agency Bazaarvoice conducted market research to find opportunities in which it could use a Transcender approach to win. (Transcender companies do conduct market research to gain customer and market insights, but they rely much less on product positioning and message testing than do Traditionalists.)

First, Lemi Shine conducted customer market research. This revealed that, while most people did not really think or care much about dishwashing detergents, there was a 10 percent minority of customers who were found to be "obsessive-compulsive cleaners" who were fastidious in their approach to washing dishes. The company generously labeled this customer segment "Clean Freaks" and focused its market efforts there. According to its marketing agency, Bazaarvoice, "The best and most obvious connection between people and Lemi Shine turned out to be a shared motivation to achieve super squeaky-clean dishes... We chose to focus communication efforts upon those with unusually strong perfectionist instincts and decided to forget about the rest. Category competitors spend millions of dollars communicating what the product is, what it has got inside, and how it works. We decided instead to focus on who it is for. We surmised that, if we could become the favorite brand of those with the highest standards and expectations, the rest of the market would follow." Notice how Lemi Shine was deliberately seeking to change the dishwashing detergent game and compel the market to follow.

Second, the company developed a Campaign Agenda and Platform that could reach, connect with, and activate these customers, not only to purchase its cleaning agents but also to proselytize on behalf of the company. Below is my summary of their Campaign Platform:

## Lemi Shine Corporate Campaign Platform

| | |
|---|---|
| **CAMPAIGN AGENDA**<br>*"Game" (≤5 words)* | **CLEAN FREAK CLEAN** |
| **CAMPAIGN C-MESSAGES**<br>*Concise communications to push the Campaign Agenda (3 max)* | • "The better-for-you brand is committed to making truly effective household cleaning products that offer a better clean every time, with plenty of peace of mind and no toxic residue left behind."<br>• Lemi Shine offers a "complete line of household cleaning products powered by 100% natural citric extracts."<br>• "Lemi Shine gets the job done with no questionable chemicals, helping you create a home that is Clean Freak Clean." |
| **CAMPAIGN CANDIDATE**<br>*Company or Brand that best fits the Campaign Agenda* | **Lemi Shine** |
| **CANDIDATE POSITIONING**<br>*Perception to be created for the Candidate in the minds of stakeholders (≤5 words)* | **Better-for-You Household Cleaning Products** |

Bazaarvoice prepared a creative brief describing the concept of Clean Freak Clean: "Lemi Shine is created for Clean Freaks by Clean Freaks, because we understand that there are people in this world who demand a higher level of clean. Who refuse to settle for cloudy dishes, spotted glasses, and cruddy cutlery.

We'll stop at nothing short of Clean Freak Clean because we're Clean Freaks too." Notice how Transcender Lemi Shine and its customers share the same desire for a Clean Freak Clean dishwashing *experience*. In contrast, Traditionalist companies focus on selling dishwashing products to customers.

The company celebrates "Clean Freaks," arguably obsessive-compulsive cleaners whom others might ridicule. For example, Lemi Shine titled a 2017 corporate press release, "Clean Freaks Rejoice: Lemi Shine Introduces New Products," which announced two novel, non-toxic cleaning products that deliver a "Clean Freak-approved Clean" to prevent stains and odors.

Lemi Shine has consistently communicated this Clean Freak Agenda. On its company website, Lemi Clean introduces its "Clean Freak Team," with each employee representing a different type of Clean Freak. For instance, Andres C. in Trade Marketing calls himself a "Clean After Yourself" Clean Freak, while Gary B., an Eastern Regional Sales Manager, claims to be a "Frank Sinatra" Clean Freak: "I do it my way."

Third, the company converted current customers into Advangelicals, so that they would not only purchase Lemi Shine products but would also convince other non-Clean Freaks to do so. In keeping with its Campaign Agenda, the company labeled these Advangelicals Clean Freaks and established a "Club Clean Freak" that encouraged consumers to join for free to get exclusive offers, such as free product and sampling opportunities, exclusive email promotions, high-value coupons, and access to special events and new product launches. As explained by Bazaarvoice, Lemi Shine's strategy was to "get on their radar, induce trial, and ultimately promote brand evangelism."

To create an Advangelical Movement, the company leveraged the other three winning Actions:

**Advantages:** Lemi Shine understood that their customers prefer cleaning products that are both safe—preferably non-toxic with natural ingredients—and powerful enough to clean thoroughly. Their household cleaning products are made from 100 percent natural citric extracts.

**Access:** Prior to launch, the company jumpstarted positive product reviews by sending samples to customers in advance. When the company released a new product called Everyday Spray, Bazaarvoice forwarded samples to its Club Clean Freak sampling community. Virtually all of them responded, resulting in dozens of reviews, with a 4.8 average rating (out of 5). "Millennials in particular are skeptical of traditional advertising tactics and product claims," said Associate Brand Manager Joel Emshoff. "By leveraging positive CGC [consumer-generated content] on our products, we're able to remove much of the apprehension consumers face when trying a new brand or product." Emshoff highlights how younger customers are becoming increasingly distrustful of Traditionalists' advertising tactics for their brands.

**Awareness:** The result of these outreach efforts was extensive consumer-generated content. Lemi Shine has distributed more than 15,000 customer reviews across retail websites, making it easier for consumers to discover its products. Here are just three of the thousands of customer reviews and comments:

*Based on this thread alone (and the fact that my glassware and black handled utensils were getting all gross) I bought some Lemi Shine yesterday, and 'used as directed.' I am not usually impressed by new products (my reaction to the iPhone in 2008: 'meh'), which is why I am enthusiastic about this. Lemi Shine does what it claims to do.*

—"SEGESTA," HOUZZ.COM (2009)

*Lemi Shine is magical. We must have the hardest water ever. Any harder and I'd be able to walk on it. Our dishes had the grossest white film on them that just kept getting thicker and grittier and grosser. I thought we were going to have to wash dishes by hand or buy new dishes. Then we tried adding Lemi Shine. No joke, after 2 or 3 cycles, the dishes look like new. I wish I had before and after pictures. Imagine an opaque drinking glass next to a crystal-clear drinking glass… I wanted to know what voodoo powder is in Lemi Shine that allows for such magical transformations to happen.*

—"AZMANAM," *CHEMISTRYBLOG.COM* (2012)

*My whole family is so excited and shocked—our glasses are absolutely crystal clear!! I can hardly believe my eyes—we had thought we would have to get a new dishwasher before the holidays, but now that plan is so happily cancelled! Excellent product and nontoxic—best combo ever!!*

—"KANDT," LEMISHINE.COM (2019)

After the campaign launched, Lemi Shine experienced 300 percent growth in site traffic, a tripling of Facebook fans, and social engagement rates double the industry average. Emshoff summarized the importance of having Advangelicals communicating the Lemi Shine Agenda and spreading the word: "As consumers continue to become more empowered with access to an abundance of information, growing brands like Lemi Shine that are disrupting the market have a significant advantage when they invest in consumer-generated content."

According to CEO Curtis Eggemeyer, privately held Lemi Shine has experienced monumental growth, with over $35 million in annual revenue in 2020. The company has only 26 employees; in comparison, its rival P&G has 99,000 employees across all its products and markets. Despite competing against gigantic brand players, Eggemeyer says, "Our demand is off the charts." He says Lemi Shine currently has "about 20 percent market share in the $150 million dishwashing detergent booster market and has sizable and growing footholds in other categories."

## CASE STUDY: GLOSSIER CO-CREATES PRODUCTS WITH ADVANGELICALS

Emily Weiss has taken the concept of Advangelicals to a whole different level. In fact, Emily was a leading social fashion influencer years before she became Founder and CEO of the cosmetic beauty products company Glossier. As a *Vogue* fashion assistant in 2010, she started a beauty blog called *Into the Gloss*. Her original focus was conventional: to write about what the "experts"—fashion leaders and celebrities—were saying and wearing.

"When I started *Into the Gloss*, I wanted to make beauty as much of an element of personal style as fashion. As I interviewed hundreds of women, I became more and more aware of how flawed the traditional beauty paradigm is. It has historically been an industry based on experts telling you, the customer, what you should or shouldn't be using on your face." Over time, however, Weiss came to an important realization: "We are all experts," she said. Weiss recognized that she could turn the fashion world upside down: instead of listening to the so-called experts, she would listen to *real* people on her blog who had real issues, insights, and ideas regarding beauty and beauty products.

That was her aha moment. Weiss decided in 2014 to use her blog to start the paradigm-shifting beauty products company Glossier, based on what she called "beauty products inspired by real life." In the process, she sought to change the fashion game: "The way I was thinking about it is, how do you make an entire beauty company based on acknowledging that everyone is their own expert? You have an opinion about beauty that someone else will probably benefit from... The fact of the matter is the majority of women today make a beauty purchasing decision based on a stranger on the internet's content."

Weiss was unique in her approach. Unlike futurists like Jobs or Musk, who envisioned products beyond the imagination of their customers, or Zara, which continuously updated its inventory based on customers' fashion suggestions, Weiss treated her bloggers as partners and experts who "co-created" products with Glossier. According to *Time* magazine, Glossier co-created Milky Jelly Face Wash based on significant input from its customers:

> Based on the hundreds of responses, Weiss and her team designed the Milky Jelly Face Wash, still Glossier's No. 1 most repurchased product. Many of their products, from lipsticks to moisturizers, have been created through crowdsourcing customer requests (after customers requested a rose-scented lip balm, the company made one), then marketed using real customers on their Instagram feed with more than 400,000 followers.

This shift, from a top-down mindset of experts telling customers what cosmetic products to use to a bottom-up approach of customers telling the company what products to make, has heralded a significant transformation in the very competitive cosmetics industry. *Vogue* magazine proclaimed that Glossier's "debut ushered in a marketing paradigm that relied on inclusive castings, natural styling, and a simple message: 'Skin first, makeup second.' The concept was revolutionary for its time, harnessing a certain come-as-you-are acceptance then new to an industry on the verge of seismic change. 'Emily's ideas have been influential to women ready to challenge the status quo—myself included,' says fashion model Karlie Kloss, who counts herself among Weiss's myriad supporters."

Weiss has transformed not only product development but also product marketing. Weiss actively cultivates and empowers Advangelicals. In a 2019 *Vox* interview, she stated, "At Glossier, something we have always stayed very true to, since pre-launch, day one, is that every single person is an influencer. I think that is so the message right now for politics, for seeing all these women going into Congress. You're really starting to understand more than ever, I think, the power of your voice and the importance of your voice, and how necessary it is to speak up."

Weiss has leveraged the Transcender political playbook to create an entire Advangelical *movement*: "Our customers are our number-one mouthpieces and evangelists. They are doing exactly what we hoped they would. They are interpreting Glossier."

Glossier now has nearly three million followers on Instagram. The company inspires these followers by offering content for their own accounts and posting photos of the followers on the Glossier account. According to *Vox*, "Everything about Glossier is designed to be photographed and talked about, from its pink bubble-wrap pouches to its interactive, hyper-designed showrooms in New York City and Los Angeles. The LA showroom, for example, has a 'canyon' room that exists to be photographed;

both locations feature mirrors with 'you look good' and 'objects are dewier than they appear' stamped on them—perfect for a mirror selfie."

Weiss says that "Instagram, for us, has been an incredible tool to show a lot of user-generated content. What we are interested in most is creating this really democratized conversation. What we do a lot of on our channel on Instagram is really celebrate people's stories. We try to find people who use Boy Brow or [another] Glossier product, but what we really want to do is evangelize that person's whole routine and all of her discoveries, whether that's a L'Oréal product or a MAC [cosmetic] product."

Some customers are so passionate that they have become one of more than 500 Glossier "Ambassadors," who each get their own web pages enabling customers to purchase the company's products. These non-company representatives receive monetary commissions and company credits. Weiss says that the Ambassador Program "emerged as a response to all the girls who want to be more involved with the brand and who were already making really incredible content around Glossier."

Here is my summary of Glossier's Campaign Platform:

## Glossier Corporate Campaign Platform

| CAMPAIGN AGENDA<br>"Game" (≤5 words) | BEAUTY PRODUCTS<br>INSPIRED BY REAL LIFE |
|---|---|
| **CAMPAIGN C-MESSAGES**<br>Concise communications<br>to push the Campaign<br>Agenda (<u>3</u> max) | • "Glossier is a new approach to beauty."<br>• Glossier co-creates products that "allow women to look like the best version of themselves, not an aspirational version of someone else."<br>• "We make intuitive, uncompli-cated products designed to live with you." |
| **CAMPAIGN CANDIDATE**<br>Company or Brand that best<br>fits the Campaign Agenda | **Glossier** |
| **CANDIDATE POSITIONING**<br>Perception to be created for<br>the Candidate in the minds<br>of stakeholders (≤5 words) | **First Socially-Driven<br>Beauty Brand** |

In this case, the Campaign Agenda and Positioning align by using the same word "beauty." In typical Transcender fashion, Glossier *leads* with the Campaign Agenda and *follows* with the "First Socially-Driven Beauty Brand" Positioning.

When Glossier was moving into its first retail store in New York City in 2016, Weiss said, "I hope that we transcend being a product company. I think product is maybe 50 percent of what we do. There's a whole other 50 percent that we offer people who are in the world of Glossier, and that's seeing the world through Glossier-colored glasses. It's an outlook. It's a certain perspective, not just product—there's far too many 'just products' in the world." This quotation perfectly summarizes the unique Transcender System: Glossier is transcending its much larger brand-focused cosmetic competitors (including Estee Lauder, L'Oréal, Coty, and many smaller rivals) and compelling the market to look through the Glossier frame of reference and play its game. The company has a Transcender mindset that recognizes it is nearly impossible to differentiate brands when there are so many me-too products on the market.

Glossier's overall Transcender approach—especially its Advangelical support—has driven the company's success. Approximately 80 percent of customers are referred to the brand by a friend, with almost 10 percent of those referrals originating from its Glossier Ambassadors Program.

In 2017, *Fast Company* named Glossier as one of its "Most Innovative Companies," while *Inc.* listed it as a "Company of the Year." According to *Forbes*, by the end of 2018 the company had been featured as a top beauty label by many leading publications, including *Teen Vogue*, *Glamour*, and *Cosmopolitan*.

Glossier currently has more than 350 employees, and operates in the United States and five other countries. The company's annual revenue more than doubled in 2018 to more than $100 million. With its latest funding by Sequoia Capital in 2019, Glossier has a market valuation exceeding $1 billion after less than four years on the market.

In a 2019 *Vox* podcast, Weiss summarized the reasons for the company's success:

We are helping to evangelize people's voices such that people can decide what they want... We think about how to give people amazing experiences. In that way, we are similar to Amazon in that we are really devoted to our customers from the standpoint that we don't want to put things into the world that are not amazing... Since we launched, we have always relied on user generation and feedback... At Glossier, we've...asked [customers]...what products to make, where to go in terms of pop-ups, or countries, and fundamentally, have been able to really change the relationship between brands and customers... [We want to create] incredible things that can really stand the test of time...and become icons in the same way that an iPhone or [an] Air Jordan [have] become essential products...

In the next chapter, I will describe the two types of buzz used to generate Transcender *Awareness*.

## CHAPTER 14 SUMMARY

- *Traditionalist companies have a mission; Transcender compa-nies are on a mission.* For many Traditionalist companies, a mission statement is often simply a statement they place on their website, whereas it represents a guiding principle for Transcenders.
- *To change the market, create an Advangelical Movement.* The most successful Transcender companies transform their Campaign Agenda into a movement of Advangelicals—missionaries who promote the company's Campaign Agenda and convert followers to push the company's Agenda by leveraging social media.
- Both Lemi Shine's Clean Freaks and Glossier's Ambassadors exemplify the impact of Advangelicals who push their respec-

tive Campaign Agendas, engage customers, and generate positive buzz, ultimately resulting in dramatically increased product sales.

# The Transcender System

**Three Techniques:**
1. Competitive Creation
2. Competitive Re-Creation
3. Competitive Categorization

I. Create

**Four Criteria:**
1. Memorable
2. Ownable
3. Winnable
4. Alignable

II. Communicate

**Four Actions:**
1. Access
2. Advantages
3. Advangelicals
4. Awareness

III. Champion

Agenda

# Awareness

The fourth way to Champion the Agenda is to create Awareness by owning the buzz. There are two types of buzz. The first is what I refer to as *bee buzz*: a relentless stream of communications akin to a bee's humming sound. This approach is designed to own the airwaves in an election and drown out the competition. Presidential candidate Donald Trump's continuous Tweeting typifies this bee buzz approach. Throughout the 2016 presidential election, Trump had multiple times the number of mentions in online and offline media that rival Hillary Clinton did.

The second type is what I refer to as *big buzz*: drumming up the most excitement on the biggest stage. For example, Senator Obama's Democratic National Convention speech in 2004 generated enormous buzz for his potential presidential bid in 2008.

I will describe these two buzz concepts in turn and explain how to apply them in the Transcender System.

## CASE STUDY: HALO TOP'S BEE BUZZ

Would you have bet money on a sweet-toothed, debt-ridden litigation lawyer who was creating his first pint of ice cream? Perhaps you should have. According to *CNBC Make It*, Halo Top founder and CEO Justin Woolverton was 33 when he became obsessed with the idea of eating a whole pint of ice cream guilt-free. Since he could not find such a thing, he decided to create it. He started in 2011 by purchasing a $20 ice cream machine on Amazon and then spent the next five years perfecting his recipe.

Woolverton was joined in this quest by another ex-lawyer and friend, Doug Bouton, who was named President and Co-Founder. At one point, the two partners were more than half a million dollars in debt, as Bouton recalls:

> We both had hundreds of thousands of dollars—more than $200,000 each, I believe—in student loan debt coming out of law school. Beyond that, Justin had five credit cards maxed out and probably something close to six figures in credit card debt. I had something like $40,000 to $50,000 in credit card debt. This was all going into the company, [but we would both] be personally bankrupt if the company failed. There was no way, no other option for either of us than declaring bankruptcy and starting over and doing something else.

In 2016, they got a lucky break: *GQ* journalist Shane Snow went on a 10-day crash diet by eating only Halo Top ice cream pints, and later published an article entitled, "What It's Like to Eat Nothing but This Magical, Healthy Ice Cream for 10 Days." Snow felt good and lost 10 pounds in the process. This propitious buzz propelled the company into the big-time. As Bouton remembered, "January 2016 is when the real hockey stick growth began. It put millions of eyeballs on the product and at the time we had the formula right, the packaging was right—it was the perfect time for that type of article to run."

The two Halo Top partners soon perfected a second recipe: social media buzz. They used several ingredients, all in line with the four winning Actions. First, they had a tremendous *Advantage*: a winning recipe. Halo Top cartons, which range from 280 to 380 calories per pint, have only 20 to 25 percent of the calories of ice cream rivals Ben & Jerry's and Häagen-Dazs. Halo Top also claims to have one-sixth the fat and carbohydrates and 25 percent more protein than typical ice cream. Most customers report that the ice cream, which comes in over 20 flavors, also has good taste despite the dramatically fewer calories, fat, and sugar. "Halo Top is the first-ever ice cream, first and foremost, that's actually good for you and actually tastes good, so it's kind of an oxymoron," says Bouton.

Second, the company gave extensive *Access* to their ice cream through virtual and real samples. Halo Top showcased online Instagram-ready images of their various pints, which often went viral.

The company strategically targeted and sent numerous coupons for ice cream samples to many social media influencers—athletes, gym trainers, and healthy-living gurus—whose followers represented potential Halo Top customers. These *Advangelicals* then blogged and raved about the "guilt-free ice cream." Bouton said, "We were constantly reaching out to people to try to get the word out about Halo Top… For us, an influencer was not some big celebrity we were going to pay $1 million. We defined it internally as somebody who had at least 1,000 followers and got 100 likes a post and a couple of comments… It was a really effective, organic strategy that built up this evangelical fanbase."

The efforts of these Advangelicals, coupled with focused Facebook, Instagram, and Twitter advertising, resulted in tremendous buzz, and dramatically higher Awareness for the company. According to the *Referral Candy Blog*, Halo Top increased its ice cream sales by 2,500 percent by implementing Transcender campaigning. Halo Top currently has over 700,000 followers on Facebook and Instagram, and over 40,000 followers on Twitter. In addition, it has received mainstream media buzz, with favorable reviews in *Spoon University*, *Buzzfeed*, and *USA Today*.

Halo Top continues to create constant bee buzz so that the company remains top of mind. For example, Halo Top sponsored a challenge with partner Scruples Hair Care to have 10 hairdressers style the hair of 10 models based on Halo Top ice cream flavors. The models posed with their pint of Halo Top ice cream and dressed to match their respective flavor for Instagram.

The Halo Top Hair results included "Rainbow Swirl" (dyed braids of rainbow colors), "Peanut Butter Cup" (dyed hair extensions with clipped golden accents), and "Birthday Cake" (multiple different colors with polka dots). The images and story were picked up in several media publications, including *Bustle*'s 2018 article "Halo Top Hair is Now a Thing and the Looks are

Actually Gorgeous." *Insider* referred to it as "Halo Top-Inspired Hair" and claimed that "the trend is sweeping ice internet."

Here is my summary of Halo Top's Corporate Campaign Platform:

## Halo Top Corporate Campaign Platform

| | |
|---|---|
| **CAMPAIGN AGENDA** *"Game"* (≤5 words) | **GUILT-FREE ICE CREAM** |
| **CAMPAIGN C-MESSAGES** Concise communications to push the Campaign Agenda (3 max) | • "Halo Top transformed the ice cream landscape with a low-calorie ice cream that provides the authentic taste and creamy texture of ice cream, without the added guilt." <br> • Halo Top "delivers premium ice cream people can actually feel good about eating." <br> • "Halo Top is crafted with only the finest ingredients while remaining high in protein and low in sugar." |
| **CAMPAIGN CANDIDATE** Company or Brand that best fits the Campaign Agenda | **Halo Top** |
| **CANDIDATE POSITIONING** Perception to be created for the Candidate in the minds of stakeholders (≤5 words) | **First-Ever 100% Natural, Low-Calorie Ice Cream** |

The Campaign Agenda of "Guilt-Free Ice Cream" harkens back to founder Justin Woolverton's desire to eat a whole pint of ice cream in a single sitting. In fact, some Halo Top containers encourage customers to "go ahead, eat the whole pint." The best Agendas have an intriguing background story that supports the overall campaign narrative, such as Obama's unique upbringing dovetailing with his Campaign Agenda of Change. Halo Top's Agenda also demonstrates Double Alignment: "ice cream" is mentioned in both the Agenda and Positioning.

By leveraging this Campaign Platform and creating consistent buzz, Halo Top has changed the ice cream game and transcended much larger corporate competitors. In July 2017, Halo Top Creamery became the best-selling pint of ice cream in America. According to the *Financial Times*, "Halo Top has become a poster child for the new reality shaking the consumer goods industry: the rise of challenger brands in everything from razors to dog food. Pitching themselves as greener, more local, more authentic or healthier than mainstream products, these upstarts often sell directly to consumers via online channels and use social media to attract attention."

Demonstrating Competitive Categorization, Halo Top effectively owns a new type of "healthy ice cream." Graeme Pitkethly, the Chief Financial Officer of Unilever, the world's largest manufacturer of ice cream brands, including Ben & Jerry's, acknowledged that the consumer brands giant "had missed the trend" in the United States for healthier ice cream, and that "Halo Top is taking share very, very quickly." According to *BBC News*, Unilever offered Woolverton $2 billion for the company in 2018. Halo Top rejected that offer but accepted an offer a year later to be acquired by Wells Enterprises, owner of Blue Bunny and other frozen treats.

Named as one of *Time* magazine's Best Inventions of 2017, Halo Top currently leads the "healthy ice cream" category. In a 2017 interview with *Ad Age*, Woolverton proclaimed, "We can't keep Halo Top on shelves, whether it's in L.A., New York, or Wyoming." Not bad for someone who started at the age of 33 by making ice cream in his kitchen!

In the next case study, I will explain how Carrie Hammer changed the fashion game with *big buzz*.

## CASE STUDY: CARRIE HAMMER'S "ROLE MODELS NOT RUNWAY MODELS" CAMPAIGN

Designer Carrie Hammer launched a fashion line in 2012, but it was not until two years later that her company truly took off. For the February 2014 New York Fashion Week ("NYFW"), the highest-profile series of fashion events in the United States, designer Carrie Hammer had two goals for her show: display her collection and change the fashion world. She did both.

As CEO of her self-named clothing brand, a line dedicated to professional women, Hammer was struggling to find the right models for her fashions: "There was no way I could use 'traditional models.'" In a 2019 *Love Happens Mag.com* article, "How Carrie Hammer is Changing the Meaning of Beauty in the Fashion Industry," she explained that "the [models] were perfect by industry standards, but there was a visual disconnect that I couldn't put my finger on… These girls are great, but the women wearing my clothes are executives and power brokers; they're role models, not runway models." This was Carrie's aha moment: she wanted "role models, not runway models" to showcase her collection.

Hammer decided to change the fashion game. She started "Role Models, Not Runway Models," a campaign replacing traditional fashion models with powerful women: activists, executives, and philanthropists. Her NYFW show also featured two historic firsts: the first wheelchair-bound model, clinical psychologist and disability rights activist Danielle Sheypuk; and the first woman with Down syndrome to walk the runway, *American Horror Story* actress Jamie Brewer. *The Huffington Post* quoted Hammer saying, "I think this challenges what we've been seeing for way too long. Uniformity. It's time to see not just diversity—but reality."

The show created a unique buzz and struck a deep chord for many women. Hammer received hundreds of thanks-filled emails, including one from Karen Crespo, a quadruple amputee who had lost both her confidence and her limbs to a systemic infection two years earlier. In a 2014 *Bustle* article, journalist Tyler Atwood reported that Crespo wrote in her email to Hammer: "I am now living my life using prosthetic arms and legs for independence. I still have a hard time dealing with my appearance. I used to have so much self-confidence, but lately I have been afraid to accept myself…"

Crespo proclaimed in a *Buzzfeed* story, "I was so thrilled and moved that a designer welcomed someone with a disability on the runway. You don't see that often and I hope it really opens doors for people with disabilities. Beauty comes in all shapes and sizes—there's absolutely no right or wrong." Hammer was so moved by Crespo's message that she invited her to walk in the upcoming fall show.

Crespo received a standing ovation while modeling Carrie Hammer's clothes at the Fall New York Fashion Week Show as she became the first quadruple amputee ever to walk that runway. *ABC News* quoted Hammer proclaiming that "Karen is going to inspire so many people. I hope she inspires the whole world."

Hammer has continued to feature other leading female role models, including entrepreneurs, business executives, scientists, activists, and philanthropists. "I think it's important that women understand that beauty comes from power, personality, and accomplishments," Hammer said. "The women we put on the runway are all at the top of their respective fields."

Since the two 2014 NYFS shows, Hammer has conducted several other fashion events in New York and Shanghai. She has said that "having the role models did distract from the clothes because the women shone so brightly while wearing them—but the distraction was part of the point." Notice how Hammer intentionally led with her Campaign Agenda of role models and followed with her branded fashions. Hammer was seeking to change the game from how women's fashions *looked* to how fashions *feel.* Her so-called Body Positive movement was not so much about the clothes as about the women who were wearing them.

Here is my summary of her Campaign Agenda and Platform:

## Carrie Hammer Corporate Campaign Platform

| CAMPAIGN AGENDA<br>"Game" (≤5 words) | ROLE MODELS NOT<br>RUNWAY MODELS |
|---|---|
| **CAMPAIGN C-MESSAGES**<br>Concise communications to push the Campaign Agenda (<u>3</u> max) | • "We believe in role models, not runway models."<br>• "Carrie Hammer provides fashion-forward, powerful clothing for professional women and a global Role Model network of high-powered women."<br>• Carrie Hammer is "kickstarting the body positive movement that has changed the way the fashion industry views beauty standards." |
| **CAMPAIGN CANDIDATE**<br>Company or Brand that best fits the Campaign Agenda | **Carrie Hammer** |
| **CANDIDATE POSITIONING**<br>*Perception to be created for the Candidate in the minds of stakeholders (≤5 words)* | **Body Positive Movement** |

In this Campaign Platform, the Positioning does not directly align or use the same wording as the Campaign Agenda. However, it supports the Agenda, because the Body Positive movement conveys that beauty is defined more by how a woman acts and feels—in a positive way with a positive self-image—than by how she looks. She and her company are on a mission "to expand the global definition of beauty beyond skin deep to include passion, purpose, and accomplishments and to empower a new generation of women to feel beautiful in their own skin."

Hammer managed to build the biggest buzz on the biggest stage. Her disruptive approach created a movement that generated over one billion media impressions. *Fox News* called it "The Runway Revolution," a fashion movement that was credited for kickstarting the body positive movement that has changed the way the fashion industry views beauty standards. By owning the stage, Hammer changed the game, the fashion industry, and the way women view themselves.

The best Transcender Campaigns create huge Awareness and ignite an Advangelical movement, often changing culture itself. As Carrie Hammer demonstrated, Transcending starts with the individual, as I will describe in the next chapter.

## CHAPTER 15 SUMMARY

- There are two types of buzz that generate **Awareness**, the fourth "A" in the Transcender System:
  - *Bee Buzz* is a relentless stream of communications, like a bee flying around all the time, akin to presidential candidate Trump's continuous tweets.
  - *Big Buzz* refers to creating the biggest buzz or excitement on the biggest stage, as did Barack Obama's 2004 DNC speech.
- Transcender Campaigns generate enormous buzz and create a powerful *movement* for change.
  - Halo Top founder and CEO Justin Woolverton perfected two recipes: "guilt-free ice cream" and social media "bee buzz." He and his co-founder Doug Bouton strategically targeted social media influencers—athletes, gym trainers, and

healthy-living gurus—whose followers represented potential Halo Top customers. These Advangelicals, coupled with focused Facebook, Instagram, and Twitter advertising, generated tremendous buzz and product sales.

- Transcender Campaigns generate enormous buzz and create a powerful *movement* for change. In 2014, designer Carrie Hammer created the biggest buzz on the biggest US fashion stage: New York Fashion Week. As CEO of her self-named clothing brand, she had two goals: to showcase her collection and change the fashion world. She did both. Hammer featured Role Models, Not Runway Models, including the first wheelchair-bound woman, the first woman with Down syndrome, and the first quadruple-amputee to walk the famous runway. Hammer founded the "Body Positive Movement" that has changed the way the fashion industry views beauty standards.

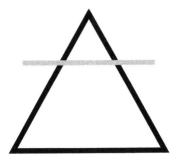

# CONCLUSION

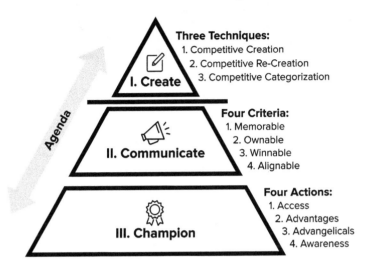

The Transcender System

**I. Create**

Three Techniques:
1. Competitive Creation
2. Competitive Re-Creation
3. Competitive Categorization

**II. Communicate**

Four Criteria:
1. Memorable
2. Ownable
3. Winnable
4. Alignable

**III. Champion**

Four Actions:
1. Access
2. Advantages
3. Advangelicals
4. Awareness

Agenda

# Applying the Transcender System

I began this book with President John F. Kennedy's "Man on the Moon" Agenda because it masterfully illustrates the three steps of the Transcender System: Create, Communicate, and Champion the Campaign Agenda. First, Kennedy created a simple, four-word Campaign Agenda: Man on the Moon. He then repeatedly and consistently communicated his Campaign Agenda with a Campaign Platform that I have summarized below:

# Kennedy's "Man on the Moon" Campaign Platform

| | |
|---|---|
| **CAMPAIGN AGENDA**<br>*"Game"* (≤5 words) | **MAN ON THE MOON** |
| **CAMPAIGN C-MESSAGES**<br>*Concise communications to push the Campaign Agenda* (<u>3</u> max) | • "This nation should commit itself to achieving the goal, before this decade is out, of landing a man on the Moon and returning him safely to the Earth."<br>• "We choose to go to the Moon...because that challenge is one that we intend to win." |
| **CAMPAIGN CANDIDATE**<br>*Company or Brand that best fits the Campaign Agenda* | **United States** |
| **CANDIDATE POSITIONING**<br>*Perception to be created for the Candidate in the minds of stakeholders* (≤5 words) | **The *First* Country to Land a Man on the Moon** |
| **COMPETITOR COUNTER-POSITIONING**<br>*Perception to be created for rivals in the minds of key stakeholders* (<5 words) | *Soviet Union: Just Space, Not Moon* |

Kennedy ultimately changed the Agenda by taking several winning Actions, including accessing the necessary financing, technologies, and professionals for NASA. Kennedy's simple, four-word Campaign Agenda made it easy for each NASA employee to understand the role he or she played to contribute to landing a "Man on the Moon."

The Transcender System provides a blueprint that *any* company can use to win. However, in my analysis of winning companies and professionals, I have found two essential characteristics of Transcender professionals that help ensure the success of this system: having a **Winning Mindset** and the ability to ensure **Winning Execution**, which I define as having a passionate commitment towards implementing the Transcender System. President Kennedy exemplified these traits during his iconic 1962 speech at Rice University:

> If I were to say, my fellow citizens, that we shall send to the moon, 240,000 miles away from the control station in Houston, a giant rocket more than 300 feet tall, the length of this football field, made of new metal alloys, some of which have not yet been invented, capable of standing heat and stresses several times more than have ever been experienced, fitted together with a precision better than the finest watch...on an untried mission, to an unknown celestial body, and then return it safely to earth, re-entering the atmosphere at speeds of over 25,000 miles per hour, causing heat about half that of the temperature of the sun... and do all this, and do it right, and do it first before this decade is out—then we must be bold.

Kennedy demonstrated a **Winning Mindset:** he had bold confidence that the US was going to win. Kennedy asked the US to accomplish many things that had never been conceived of in the history of mankind, including using materials not yet created. Kennedy was confident that NASA would achieve this herculean task in an incredibly tight timeframe. To ensure **Winning Execution**, he needed to win public support to secure the resources to make it happen. Only four months after becoming President, Kennedy submitted a space budget that exceeded the space budgets of the previous eight years combined. The Rice University speech won over the public.

The proof of these attributes is in the historical record. Despite Kennedy's assassination, the Apollo 1 fire which killed three astronauts, and several other setbacks, NASA was committed to and ultimately fulfilled Kennedy's Campaign Agenda of landing a man on the moon.

## THE TRANSCENDER WINNING MINDSET

Kennedy's winning mentality is characteristic of many of the Transcender professionals I have highlighted in this book. For example, Elon Musk has been bold in his very public Campaign Agenda to "transition the world to sustainable energy" by producing compelling mass-market electric cars. Despite many naysayers, Musk created the most valuable car company in the world.

Similarly, Steve Jobs believed that his company could reimagine the cellphone, develop the first successful tablet PC in nearly three decades, and revolutionize the way people listen to music. Jobs' confidence and inspiration led Apple to accomplish all of those feats. Carrie Hammer shocked the fashion world with her bold idea to showcase role models—including real-world female executives, a woman in a wheelchair, and a quadruple amputee—instead of runway models. Seedlip's Ben Branson and Halo Top's Justin Woolverton were both willing to leave safe, lucrative jobs to invest their time and money to create game-changing products that had never previously existed.

The Winning Mindset starts with winning leaders. In my consulting experience, I have found that the best Transcender companies have executives and other professionals at *all levels* of the company who commit to, believe in, communicate, and push their company's Campaign Agenda, both within and outside of their organization. These Transcender professionals are change agents who inspire their colleagues to set out on a mission to win on behalf of their customers. They do not follow or react; they lead and "proact."

Transcender professionals do not think the way Traditionalists do. In his last annual shareholder letter as the CEO of Amazon, Jeff Bezos wrote to his employees,

> I have one last thing of utmost importance I feel compelled to teach. I hope all Amazonians take it to heart… In what ways does the world pull at you in an attempt to make you normal? How much work does it take to maintain your distinctiveness? To keep alive the thing or things that make you special?… We all know that distinctiveness—originality—is valuable. We are all taught to 'be yourself.' What I'm really asking you to do is to embrace and be realistic about how much energy it takes to maintain that distinctiveness. The world wants you to be typical—in a thousand ways, it pulls at you. **Don't let it happen.**

The Transcender professional, unlike the Traditionalist professional, does not see fences; he or she sees fields. The Transcender professional does not see threats; he or she sees opportunities. While the Traditionalist professional finds excuses (e.g., too little time, money, resources) for losing, the Transcender professional finds pathways to *winning*.

## THE TRANSCENDER WINNING EXECUTION

Jeff Bezos is passionate about virtually every detail to ensure that

Amazon's employees and partners are customer obsessed (e.g., product orders must exceed 99 percent accuracy). The Sweetgreen team has worked diligently to ensure that its products are farm-fresh and identified by the producing farm. And Starbucks employees, from the CEO to the baristas, are committed to making sure all of its customers experience "The Third Place."

Transcender professionals win by *prioritizing* and *focusing*. Transcender professionals do not treat all Actions equally; they eliminate some traditional tactics that do not align with their Agenda and will go deep on those Actions that do. They focus only on those winning Actions and supporting activities that will push their Campaign Agenda. In my experience, I have found that Transcender professionals generally have 20 to 30 percent less work and significantly more free time because they are so focused on only those actions that will help their organizations win. For them, less is more.

Moreover, Transcender professionals recognize the importance of speed. Unlike more analytical and risk-averse Traditionalist professionals, Transcender professionals act fast: they quickly analyze their competitive situation and take actions in the marketplace to win. They do not wait for all of the competitive data or market information to come in; they move based on limited data because they understand how quickly markets change.

Transcender professionals also feel a sense of *urgency*. They realize that every day their "voters"—their customers and stakeholders—are making up their minds about products. As a result, they seek the practical, not the perfect, answer, and take decisive action.

In my consulting engagements, I am often surprised by which

professionals at a particular company think and act like winning Transcender leaders. You do <u>not</u> have to be a CEO or senior executive to be a winning Transcender leader. Winning Transcender leaders can be found at all corporate levels, functions, disciplines, markets, and locations—not only seasoned professionals but also new hires; not only in marketing, sales, commercial, and communication, but also in research, product design, finance, and throughout the supply chain. All a Transcender needs is the passionate commitment to thinking and acting boldly.

## APPLYING THE TRANSCENDER SYSTEM

So how do you apply the Transcender System at your company right away? You can start by leveraging the powerful, proven Transcender System using three practical steps: Create, Communicate, and Champion the Campaign Agenda.

I recommend that you begin by sharing the Transcender System concepts with your business colleagues, and preferably your product, function, or local market team. Explain that leading companies get their products elected like US presidential candidates. They create and communicate a single, overarching Campaign Agenda that is memorable (five words or fewer), ownable, winnable, and alignable. Share with your team some notable examples from this book, such as Starbucks, Apple, or Nike. **Emphasize that these Transcender companies lead with their Campaign Agenda and follow with their brand.**

First, **Create the Agenda**.

Second, **Communicate the Agenda**. Encourage your team to prepare a Campaign Platform to flesh out the most important messaging: the Campaign Agenda, C-Messages, Positioning, P-Bites, and the Counter-Positioning of competitors. I have included a copy of the Campaign Platform template below. You can also download a copy of the Transcender System Campaign Platform template at **www.DrStanBernard.com**.

| The Transcender System™: Campaign Platform Template | |
| --- | --- |
| **CAMPAIGN AGENDA** <br> *"Game" (≤5 words)* | |
| **CAMPAIGN C-MESSAGES** <br> *Concise communications to push the Campaign Agenda (<u>3</u> max)* | |
| **CAMPAIGN CANDIDATE** <br> *Company or Brand that best fits the Campaign Agenda* | |
| **CANDIDATE POSITIONING** <br> *Perception to be created for the Candidate in the minds of stakeholders (≤5 words)* | |
| **COMPETITOR COUNTER-POSITIONING** <br> *Perception to be created for rivals in the minds of key stakeholders (<5 words)* | |

Third, **Champion the Agenda.** Discuss and brainstorm ways that your team and company can win with the four **Actions** I have described in this book. Seek to address these four questions:

- *How can your company grant Access in order to gain competitive advantage?* Access can be designed to be either limited or unlimited, such as Zara's fast fashions or Google's search information. Remember that Access can mean offering greater value even if your product is higher priced, such as Starbucks' coffee or Peloton's Bike.
- *What Advantages does your product offer?* These Advantages may be product related or extend beyond the product itself. For example, many people have purchased Tesla's cars not only because of their many unique features but also because they fervently believe in and support the company's Campaign Agenda: to accelerate the "World's Transition to Sustainable Energy."
- *How can your company create an Advangelical movement for the corporation or its products?* Can your company engage and energize product "Ambassadors" like those Glossier created? What about generating numerous positive consumer reviews, as Lemi Shine did for its non-toxic Clean Freak Clean products?
- *How can your company create game-changing Awareness by producing bee buzz or big buzz?* Remember how tiny Halo Top engaged social media influencers, including journalists, gym trainers, and healthy-living gurus, to drum up excitement for its "guilt-free ice cream"? They even arranged for Scruple's hairstylists to create "Halo Top Hair" styles, producing memorable photos that went viral. Can your company create or steal a high-profile event, as Carrie Hammer did with her "Role Models, Not Runway Models" Campaign Agenda?

I have profiled 16 companies in *Brands Don't Win*, including Google, Amazon, Uber, Seedlip, and GEICO. Like your company, they all started winning, <u>not</u> with their brand, but with a simple, five-words-or-fewer *Campaign Agenda*. These Transcenders relentlessly communicated their Agenda and Campaign Platform to inspire their stakeholders and customers to join their election campaign. Using a political playbook, they pushed their Campaign Agenda with four winning Actions to generate unique Access, distinct Advantages, huge Awareness, and an Advangelical following. By leveraging the Transcender System, each of these leading companies has transcended the brand game to play a new game only they could win.

So what kind of game do you want to play? The opportunity is yours; you get to decide. You don't have to send a man to the moon to become a Transcender. By following the Transcender System, any company, in any industry, can create the terms of their own game to win!

## CHAPTER 16 SUMMARY

- There are two important attributes of Transcender leaders to ensure the success of the Transcender System: having a **Winning Mindset** and ensuring **Winning Execution**.
- President John F. Kennedy demonstrated these two characteristics with his Man on the Moon Campaign Agenda. First, he expressed and demonstrated bold confidence that the US was going to win. With the lunar mission, Kennedy asked the US to accomplish many things that had never been conceived of in the history of mankind. Kennedy's Winning Mentality is a key trait of many Transcender professionals. Second, Kennedy and his NASA team displayed Winning Execution: they had a passionate commitment to implement the Campaign Agenda of landing a man on the moon despite overwhelming odds and numerous setbacks.

- Like Kennedy, Transcender professionals win by prioritizing and focusing. They focus only on those winning Actions and supporting activities that will push their Campaign Agenda.
- Transcender companies have executives and other professionals at *all levels* who commit to, believe in, communicate, and push the Campaign Agenda. They are change agents who inspire their colleagues to set out on a mission to win on behalf of their customers.
- You can start applying the powerful, proven Transcender System at your company right away by using three practical steps: **Create, Communicate, and Champion the Campaign Agenda**. Work with your business colleagues to create and communicate a single, overarching Campaign Agenda.
- Prepare a **Campaign Platform** to communicate the most important messaging: the Campaign Agenda, C-Messages, Candidate, Positioning, P-Bites, and the Counter-Positioning of competitors.
- Finally, discuss and brainstorm ways that your team and company can win with the four types of **Actions** I have described in this book. By following the Transcender System, any company, in any industry, can create the terms of their own game to win!

# About the Author

**Stan Bernard, MD, MBA** is an internationally recognized, award-winning global competition consultant, keynote speaker, and published author. He is president of Bernard Associates, LLC, and the creator of the Transcender System™. He has been featured on television and in leading publications, including the *Wall Street Journal, Business 2.0*, and *Businessweek*. Dr. Bernard has published over 75 book chapters, syndicated reports, and articles.

For nearly four decades, Dr. Bernard has consulted with over a dozen Fortune 500 firms and 150 other leading companies spanning six continents. He has been involved in more than 300 product launches involving more than 60 countries. Over 15,000 professionals have participated in his firm's Competitive Simulations ("business war games"), Transcender System Training Workshops, Transcender System Seminars, and speaking engagements.

As a Senior Fellow at The Wharton School, Dr. Bernard taught marketing to MBA students for 14 years. He has conducted numerous presentations at executive business meetings, professional societies, government agencies, and academic institutions, including the Stanford Graduate School of Business, Columbia Business School, Harvard University School of Public Health, and the Northwestern University Kellogg Business School.

Dr. Bernard received his MBA in marketing and healthcare management from the Wharton School of Business. He received his Medical Degree from Baylor College of Medicine and was previously a licensed general practitioner. He received his BA in the Biological Basis of Behavior from the University of Pennsylvania and completed additional coursework at Edinburgh University in Scotland.

Dr. Bernard has served on the boards of numerous companies, journals, and organizations, including Morristown Medical Center (New Jersey), the New York Chapter of the Healthcare Businesswomen's Association, and the Dorothy B. Hersh Foundation, which provides grants to help special needs children in New Jersey.

# Acknowledgments

*"It takes a village to bring a book into the world, as everyone who has written one knows. Many people have helped me to complete this one, sometimes without even knowing it. They are so numerous that I will not even attempt to acknowledge them individually, for fear that I might leave one out."*

—HILLARY CLINTON, IT TAKES A VILLAGE: AND
OTHER LESSONS CHILDREN TEACH US

I also found that it took a village to write *Brands Don't Win*. My "village" started with my first two consulting clients in 1985 and has grown exponentially since then. Over 150 client companies and 15,000 professionals have experienced, pressure-tested, and helped me enhance the Transcender System. I am grateful for all their insights, suggestions, and encouragement to optimize this winning approach. I sincerely hope this book will further their understanding and application of the system to help them and their companies win.

Not many authors benefit from the sage counsel and editing expertise of a Pulitzer Prize winner, best-selling author, and former *Washington Post* reporter, but I did from my life-long friend David Vise. I really appreciated his assistance with the book editing and cover design. My son Brian Bernard conducted a very thorough and valuable review of the book. His high-level strategic analysis and detailed editing enhanced my early drafts.

Several other reviewers contributed to the book. I was initially reluctant but ultimately submitted my manuscript for "grading" from two of my kids' former teachers, Randi and Peter Schmidt. Fortunately, they gave me their keen perspectives and a high grade. Kathleen Tregoning provided her valuable perspectives as both a former political advisor and current business executive. Two of my earliest reviewers, Sid Mazel and Evan Meiselman, were brave enough to offer their feedback.

Micheline and Francois Nader provided me with valuable encouragement and support throughout my writing process. I am grateful to Richard Brooks for serving both as a sounding board and chapter reviewer. Friends and book authors David Shulkin and Carol Cassella gave me helpful information on publishing a book. Liani Wang suggested several ideas for case studies, and Tom Reynolds provided excellent marketing suggestions.

I want to thank the valued team members of my Bernard Associates consulting firm who not only have assisted and supported my company but also have traveled, eaten, and laughed with me across the globe: Ashley Nedd, Jennifer Martineau, Victoria Behr, Allison Conway, Cecilia Kim, Andrea Berkow, Janet Wells, Ben Shapiro, Cheryl Marchese, Jana Bernard, Mareike Schmidt, Katie Grabowski, Peter Grabowski, Xio Curry, Judi Francus, Cassandra Mayberry, and Sydnie Bruekner.

To write a book about winning, I required a publisher with a winning team and process. I found that at Scribe Media. My editor Emma Rosenburg successfully challenged and helped me to take my book game up to a whole new level. I had the honor to work with many other Scribe experts, including Katie Orr, Skyler White, Rachel Brandenburg, Alexa Davis, Annaliese Hoehling, Ingrid Bartinique, Miles Rote, Erin Michele Sky, Rikki Jump, Geoff Pope, Areil Sutton, Jordan Grenadier, and several others.

Finally, I want to thank the readers of *Brands Don't Win*. I sincerely hope this book helps you, your products, and your company WIN!

# Glossary

*Advangelicals*: The best presidential campaigns—and product campaigns—create an overwhelming movement of Advangelicals: political and corporate campaign supporters who advocate, advise, promote, support, and push the Campaign Agenda.

*Campaign Agenda*: The core, overarching concept that a candidate wants to convey to constituents, or that a company seeks to communicate to its key stakeholders. It is also the "game" a political candidate or a company wants to force its rivals to play. For example, Senator Barack Obama's 2008 presidential election Campaign Agenda was Change; Amazon's Campaign Agenda is Customer Obsession.

*Creating the Agenda*: Politicians, especially during elections, often shape the narrative of an election by Creating the Campaign Agenda or "game." For example, President John F. Kennedy and the US won the Space Race by changing the game to the "Man on the Moon" Race. Companies similarly Create the Agenda: Starbucks transformed and dominated the coffee shop business by executing its Campaign Agenda of The Third Place between home and work in America.

*Competitive Categorization*: Finding and/or owning a new, distinct product category. For example, Apple did not initiate but ultimately owned a third category of devices with the iPad, which was neither a personal computer nor a cellphone.

*Competitive Creation*: Creating an entirely new market space for a product. Apple's iPod, in combination with the digital iTunes music system, illustrates Competitive Creation.

*Campaign Platforms*: Politicians and Transcender companies leverage concise communications called Campaign Platforms to encourage their stakeholders to buy in, support, and repeat these communications. Transcender Platforms typically include the Campaign Agenda, Campaign Messages (C-Messages), the Candidate, the Candidate Positioning, Product Bites (P-Bites), and the Counter-Positioning of competitors.

*C-Messages*: Campaign messages designed to help push and communicate the Campaign Agenda. Typically, they use short phrases to repeat the key word(s) from the Campaign Agenda, such as Obama's C-Messages: "Change We Can Believe In," "Yes, We Can," and "Change and Hope."

*Candidate Positioning*: How the political team or company influences the perception of their candidate or product in the minds of their constituents/stakeholders. Candidate Positioning differs from traditional product positioning by typically incorporating word(s) from the Campaign Agenda. For example, Obama's Campaign Team *positioned*, or created the perception of, Obama as the Change Candidate, which directly aligned with his overarching Agenda for Change. Unlike traditional product positioning statements, Transcender Positioning is five words or fewer.

*Champion the Agenda*: The third and final step in the Transcender System is Champion the Agenda. Transcenders force competitors to play their game by leveraging the four types of winning Actions: Access, Advantages, Advangelicals, and Awareness.

*Communicate the Agenda*: This is the second step in the Transcender System. Transcender companies leverage concise communications called Campaign Platforms to encourage their stakeholders to buy in, support, and repeat these communications. The Campaign Platform incorporates the Campaign Agenda and other key communications into one single, succinct page.

*Competitive Measure*: To be successful, Transcender companies change the game, which means they often change how the game is measured. The Competitive Measure is the new metric the company wants to be evaluated on. For example, Amazon does not prioritize the traditional measures of corporate sales and profitability but rather customer engagement metrics, which directly align with its overall Campaign Agenda of "Customer Obsession."

*Competitor Counter-Positioning*: The perception a politician or company wants to create for their rival or their rival's products in the minds of their stakeholders.

*Competitive Re-Creation*: Creating a game-changing product by reimagining an existing product (e.g., the cellphone). The iPhone demonstrates the concept of Competitive Re-Creation.

*Double Alignment*: When the Positioning of the candidate or product uses the same word or wording as the Campaign Agenda.

*Multi-Level Competition*: In the Transcender System, companies can compete at four different levels: the brand level (e.g., a particular generation of iPhone); the franchise level (the entire iPhone franchise, including previous and current iPhone models); the portfolio level (Apple's portfolio of products); and the corporate level (the perception of Apple as a corporation by employees, customers, and stakeholders). Most companies seek to compete on the level or level(s) that best provide competitive advantage.

*Paradigm Shift*: A paradigm shift occurs when there is a crisis in a particular field, and the old paradigm can no longer account for enough of the existing evidence. Eventually, the old view is replaced by the new view, because it is a better approximation to reality. Notably, a paradigm shift is a dramatic change: it is a *revolution*, not an evolution.

*P-Bites*: Instead of numerous brand messages, the Transcender companies use two or three "Product bites" or "P-Bites," each typically five words or fewer, to describe their products. P-Bites effectively replace longer brand messages in the Transcender System because they are more memorable.

*Play Your Game*: "Play Your Game" occurs when a company identifies or creates a competitive situation where it sets the rules, forces competitors to react, and ultimately gains significant competitive advantage(s) in its market(s). Companies that play their game usually win the game.

*Political Playbook*: Transcender companies win by "Changing the Agenda" or forcing competitors to play their game. They conduct election-style campaigns to commercialize their products. Like US presidential campaigns, these companies take three steps: 1) Create the Agenda, 2) Communicate the Agenda, and 3) Champion the Agenda.

*Product*: For the purposes of this book, I define "product" as products, goods, services, technologies, and other offerings.

*Product Playbook*: Traditionalist companies commercialize their products using a military-style campaign. Their goal is two-fold: 1) to win by differentiating their product brand based on superior features and benefits, and 2) to overwhelm competitors with significantly greater investments and better promotional tactics.

*Stakeholders*: Stakeholders can include product pundits or experts, financial and market analysts, journalists and other media representatives, big-name partners and purchasers, consumer influencers or bloggers, and others. These powerful constituencies are analogous to the Electoral College delegates in US presidential elections. Presidential candidates know that they must win the Electoral College vote—not the popular vote—to become President. Similarly, Transcender companies recognize that they must win over their stakeholders since they are so influential on customers.

*Traditionalists*: Companies that use old, conventional marketing approaches to compete. These companies try to win by differentiating their product brand, the same game that has been played by most companies—in some cases, for centuries. Traditionalists also apply the standard 4 P's (Product, Place, Promotion, and Price) of marketing to win. Traditionalists typically are compelled to play and react to a Transcender's game.

*Transcenders*: Companies that have risen above and surpassed

Traditionalists competitors by using more of a political play-book rather than a product playbook. These companies do not win by differentiating their brands; they win by Changing the Agenda, forcing competitors to play their game. Significantly, these companies win by communicating and championing a simple, concise "Campaign Agenda."

*The Transcender System*™: A unique, three-step framework based on US presidential elections which is designed to help a company shape its market to win. The three steps are 1) Create the Agenda, 2) Communicate the Agenda, and 3) Champion the Agenda. Importantly, the Transcender System is not a marketing department approach; it is a company-wide approach.

*Triple Alignment*: When the Positioning of the candidate or product and the competitive measure use the same word or wording as the Campaign Agenda.

*Winning Actions*: Actions are cross-functional, multi-disciplinary, and cross-geographic activities designed to push the company's Campaign Agenda. These Actions are based on the 4 A's: *Access*, *Advantages*, *Advangelicals*, and *Awareness*.

# Bibliography

## INTRODUCTION

*Best Global Brands 2019.* (New York: Interbrand, 2019), https://www. interbrand.com/wp-content/uploads/2019/10/Interbrand_Best_Global_ Brands_2019.pdf.

Gasper, Christopher L. "Nick Saban and Bill Belichick Are Kindred Souls." *The Boston Globe,* January 7, 2017, https://www.bostonglobe.com/ sports/patriots/2017/01/07/nick-saban-and-bill-belichick-are-kindred-souls/oUmAptRUZg2DqRxI8khGFP/story.html.

"John R. Wooden's Pyramid of Success." UCLA Athletics, accessed April 16, 2021, https://uclabruins.com/sports/2013/4/17/208274583.aspx.

Logsdon, John M. "John F. Kennedy and NASA." *NASA,* May 22, 2015, https://www.nasa.gov/feature/john-f-kennedy-and-nasa.

Lopresto, Mike. "It's Been 50 Years since UCLA's Historic 88-Game Win Streak." *NCAA,* January 28, 2021, https:// www.ncaa.com/news/basketball-men/article/2021-01-28/ its-been-50-years-uclas-historic-88-game-win-streak.

Saban, Nick and Brian Curtis. *How Good Do You Want to Be?* (New York: Ballantine Books, 2007).

Savage, Phil and Ray Glier. *4th and Goal Every Day* (New York: St. Martin's Press, 2017).

Schwartz, Geoff. "Here's What 'Do Your Job' Really Means for the Patriots," *SBNation*, January 26, 2017, https://www.sbnation.com/2017/1/26/14390366/patriots-do-your-job-mantra-super-bowl-2017-what-it-means.

Shouler, Kenneth. "The Streak that Won't Be Broken," ESPN, accessed April 9, 2021, https://www.espn.com/espn/page2/story?page=shouler/061128.

"Space Program," John F. Kennedy Presidential Library and Museum, accessed July 16, 2020, https://www.jfklibrary.org/learn/about-jfk/jfk-in-history/space-program.

"Sputnik Moment," Wikipedia, last modified September 29, 2019, https://en.wiktionary.org/wiki/Sputnik_moment.

"To the Moon!" Eber Leadership Group, accessed June 21, 2021, https://www.kareneber.com/blog/tothemoon.

"What does 'Sputnik moment' mean?" UsingEnglish.com, accessed July 16, 2019, https://www.usingenglish.com/reference/idioms/sputnik+moment.html.

## CHAPTER 1

"10 Oldest Companies in the World," Oldest.org, accessed March 2, 2021, https://www.oldest.org/technology/companies.

Desjardins, Jeff. "How much data is generated each day?" *World Economic Forum*, April 17, 2019, https://www.weforum.org/agenda/2019/04/how-much-data-is-generated-each-day-cf4bddf29f.

"Duracell vs. Energizer," Diffen, accessed February 27, 2021, https://www.diffen.com/difference/Duracell_vs_Energizer.

Finn, Andrew. "Paradigms and Paradigm Shifts," George Mason University, accessed June 21, 2021, http://mason.gmu.edu/~afinn/html/teaching/ courses/UMD_comm470/readings/ar1-paradigms.htm.

Geyser, Werner. "What is an Influencer?" *Influencer Marketing Hub*, last modified June 14, 2021, https://influencermarketinghub.com/ what-is-an-influencer.

"History of the Internet," Wikipedia, accessed June 17, 2020, https:// en.wikipedia.org/wiki/History_of_the_Internet.

Holland, Taylor. "What Is Branding? A Brief History." *Skyword*, August 11, 2017, https://www.skyword.com/contentstandard/ branding-brief-history.

Khan, Saif Ullah and Owais Mufti. "The Hot History and Cold Future of Brands." *Journal of Managerial Sciences* 1 (January 2007): 75–84, https://www.researchgate.net/ publication/235937759_The_Hot_History_and_Cold_Future_of_Brands.

Kuhn, Thomas S. *The Structure of Scientific Revolutions*, 2nd Ed. (Chicago: University of Chicago, 1970).

Law, Thomas J. "The Beginner's Guide to 7 Types of Internet Marketing." *Oberlo*, November 21, 2018, https://www.oberlo.com/blog/ beginners-guide-7-types-internet-marketing.

Martin, Marci. "Founded When? America's Oldest Companies." *Business News Daily*, September 28, 2018, https://www.businessnewsdaily. com/8122-oldest-companies-in-america.html.

McIntyre, Douglas A. "America's Oldest Brands," *24/7 Wall St.*, August 17, 2012, https://247wallst.com/investing/2012/08/17/ americas-oldest-brands/3.

Moore, Karl and Susan Reid. "The Birth of Brand: 4000 Years of Branding." *Business History* 50, no. 4 (June 19, 2008): 419–32, https://doi. org/10.1080/00076790802106299.

Petrov, Christo. "25+ Impressive Big Data Statistics for 2020," *TechJury*, July 1, 2020, https://techjury.net/stats-about/big-data-statistics.

Rabideau, Camryn. "16 Amazon Products with Over 15K Reviews—and Why People Love Them," *Reviewed*, May 24, 2018, https://www.reviewed.com/home-outdoors/features/16-amazing-amazon-products-with-over-15k-reviews.

Simpson, Jon. "Finding Brand Success in The Digital World." *Forbes*, August 25, 2017, https://www.forbes.com/sites/forbesagencycouncil/2017/08/25/finding-brand-success-in-the-digital-world.

"Spherical Earth," Wikipedia, accessed June 20, 2020, https://en.wikipedia.org/wiki/Spherical_Earth.

## CHAPTER 2

"2004 Democratic National Convention Keynote Address." Wikipedia, accessed on June 10, 2020, https://en.wikipedia.org/wiki/2004_Democratic_National_Convention_keynote_address.

"2008 New Hampshire Democratic Presidential Primary." Wikipedia, accessed June 24, 2020, https://en.wikipedia.org/wiki/2008_New_Hampshire_Democratic_presidential_primary.

"2008 Presidential Campaign Financial Activity Summarized: Receipts Nearly Double 2004 Total." Federal Election Commission, June 8, 2009, https://www.fec.gov/updates/2008-presidential-campaign-financial-activity-summarized-receipts-nearly-double-2004-total.

Arnon, Ben. "How the Obama 'Hope' Poster Reached a Tipping Point and Became a Cultural Phenomenon: An Interview with the Artist Shepard Fairey." *The Huffington Post*, November 13, 2008, https://www.huffpost.com/entry/how-the-obama-hope-poster_b_133874.

"Barack Obama 2008 Presidential Campaign." Wikipedia, accessed June 27, 2020, https://en.wikipedia.org/wiki/Barack_Obama_2008_presidential_campaign.

"Barack Obama Quotes." Notable Quotes, accessed June 22, 2021, http://www.notable-quotes.com/o/obama_barack.html.

"Barack Obama Quote: Your Voice Can Change the World." AZ Quotes, accessed June 22, 2021, https://www.azquotes.com/quote/543496.

Bernard, Stan. "The Permanent Campaign." *Pharmaceutical Executive*, October 1, 2011, 60–64, https://bernardassociatesllc.com/wp-content/uploads/2016/09/PermanentCampaign-SBernard21.pdf.

Berry, Mary Frances and Josh Gottheimer. "The Story Behind Obama's Keynote Address at the 2004 Democratic National Convention." *Beacon Broadside*, July 27, 2016, https://www.beaconbroadside.com/broadside/2016/07/the-story-behind-obamas-keynote-address-at-the-2004-democratic-national-convention.html.

Burden, Barry C. and Kenneth R. Mayer. "Voting Early, but Not So Often." *The New York Times*, October 24, 2010, https://www.nytimes.com/2010/10/25/opinion/25mayer.html.

Candaele, Kerry. "Barack Obama and Sam Cooke on Election Night." *The Huffington Post*, December 8, 2008, https://www.huffpost.com/entry/barack-obama-and-sam-cook_b_141895.

Cooper, Michael. "McCain Laboring to Hit Right Note on the Economy." *The New York Times*, September 16, 2008, https://www.nytimes.com/2008/09/17/us/politics/17mccain.html.

Dahl, Melissa. "Youth Vote May Have Been Key in Obama's Win." *CNBC*, November 5, 2008, http://www.nbcnews.com/id/27525497/ns/politics-decision_08/t/youth-vote-may-have-been-key-obamas-win.

Edsall, Thomas B. "The Way It Really Works." *The New Republic*, July 14, 2010, https://newrepublic.com/article/75617/the-way-it-ireallyi-works.

Fitzgerald, Thomas. "A Historic Victory for Obama." *The Philadelphia Inquirer*, November 5, 2008, https://www.inquirer.com/philly/news/homepage/20081105_HISTORIC_WIN.html.

"Fundraising for the 2008 United States Presidential Election." Wikipedia, accessed April 16, 2020, https://en.wikipedia.org/wiki/Fundraising_for_the_2008_United_States_presidential_election.

Hodges, Adam. "'Yes, We Can' and the Power of Political Slogans." *Anthropologie News*, October 21, 2019, https://www.anthropology-news.org/index.php/2019/10/21/yes-we-can-and-the-power-of-political-slogans.

MacAskill, Ewen. "US Election: McCain Tries to Steal Message of Change from Obama, but Delivery Falls Flat." *The Guardian*, September 4, 2008, https://www.theguardian.com/world/2008/sep/05/uselections2008.johnmccain2.

"Obama Spells Out Plans for Change." *CNN*, August 29, 2008, https://www.cnn.com/2008/POLITICS/08/29/obama.promises/index.html.

Rosentiel, Tom. "Young Voters in the 2008 Election." *Pew Research Center*, November 13, 2008, https://www.pewresearch.org/2008/11/13/young-voters-in-the-2008-election.

"Sam Cooke's Swan Song of Protest." *NPR*, December 16, 2007, https://www.npr.org/templates/story/story.php?storyId=17267529.

Saul, Michael. "Stunned Barack Obama Loses Luster." *New York Daily News*, January 9, 2008, https://www.nydailynews.com/news/politics/stunned-barack-obama-loses-luster-article-1.342384.

Sepulvado, John. "Obama's 'Overnight Success' in 2004 Was a Year in the Making." *Oregon Public Broadcasting*, May 19, 2016, https://www.opb.org/news/series/election-2016/president-barack-obama-2004-convention-speech-legacy.

Smith, Ben and Jonathan Martin. "Why Obama Won." *Politico*, November 5, 2008, https://www.politico.com/story/2008/11/why-obama-won-015301.

"Speech Analysis of Barack Obama at Democratic National Convention (2004)." Slideshare.net, last modified October 28, 2016, https://www.slideshare.net/shreysoni/speech-analysis-of-barack-obama.

Stirland, Sarah. "Obama's Secret Weapons: Internet, Databases and Psychology." *Wired*, October 29, 2008, https://www.wired.com/2008/10/obamas-secret-w.

Wenner, Jann S. "How Obama Won: Two leading political experts on the historic election—and how it could usher in 'a brand-new nation.'" *Rolling Stone*, November 27, 2008, https://www.rollingstone.com/politics/politics-news/how-obama-won-42930.

"Why Our Country Needs to Get Back to the Constitution." *The Whittier Daily News*, last modified August 29, 2017, https://www.whittierdailynews.com/2011/09/15/why-our-country-needs-to-get-back-to-the-constitution.

## CHAPTER 3

"#MAGA." *#MoveMe: A Guide to Social Movements and Social Media*, accessed December 21, 2020, https://moveme.berkeley.edu/project/maga.

Allen, Jonathan and Amie Parnes. *Shattered: Inside Hillary Clinton's Doomed Campaign* (New York: Crown Publishing Group, 2018).

Barry, Aoife. "What made Trump's 'Make America Great Again' slogan so powerful?" *TheJournal.ie*, November 9, 2016, https://www.thejournal.ie/trump-slogan-make-america-great-again-3071552-Nov2016.

"Bill Clinton Forgets Hillary's Campaign Slogan." Grabien, October 25, 2016, https://grabien.com/story.php?id=69951.

Carroll, Lauren. "Hillary Clinton's Top 10 Campaign Promises." *PolitiFact*, July 22, 2016, https://www.politifact.com/article/2016/jul/22/hillary-clintons-top-10-campaign-promises.

"Cognitive Framing." *Tactical Reality Dictionary*, accessed June 25, 2021, http://world-information.org/trd/06.

Cowan, Nelson. Curators' Distinguished Professor of Psychological Sciences at the University of Missouri, Personal communication, September 14, 2020.

Dias, Elizabeth. "Biden and Trump Say They're Fighting for America's 'Soul.' What Does That Mean?" *The New York Times*, October 17, 2020, https://www.nytimes.com/2020/10/17/us/biden-trump-soul-nation-country.html.

"Donald Trump on Twitter—2009/2020 Analysis." TweetBinder, accessed July 26, 2020, https://www.tweetbinder.com/blog/trump-twitter.

Dreher, Sarah. "A History of Terrible Campaign Slogans from We Polked You in '44 to Build Back Better." *Newsweek*, October 23, 2020, https://www.newsweek.com/history-terrible-campaign-slogans-we-polked-you-44-build-back-better-1541447.

Gladwell, Malcolm. *David and Goliath: Underdogs, Misfits, and the Art of Battling Giants* (New York: Little, Brown and Company: 2013).

"Hillary Clinton: Five Things We Learnt from What Happened." *The Week*, September 18, 2017, https://www.theweek.co.uk/88232/hillary-clinton-blames-bernie-sanders-for-lasting-damage.

Isenstadt, Alex. "The Week that Shook the Trump Campaign." *Politico*, July 2, 2002, https://www.politico.com/news/2020/07/02/the-week-that-shook-that-trump-campaign-348383.

Johnson, Shontavia. "Donald Trump Tweeted Himself into the White House." *The Conversation*, November 10, 2016, https://theconversation.com/donald-trump-tweeted-himself-into-the-white-house-68561.

Kelly, Ryan. "Cristiano Ronaldo vs Lionel Messi: Who is the GOAT in football? The Stats Head-to-Head Showdown." *Goal*, last modified May 27, 2021, https://www.goal.com/en-in/news/cristiano-ronaldo-vs-lionel-messi-who-is-the-goat-football-stats-/ual7d33i8hjz14plhwkf2yvkr.

Linsky, Anne. "Hillary Clinton's Campaign Message Keeps Evolving." *The Boston Globe*, May 16, 2016, http://www.bostonglobe.com/news/politics/2016/05/30/hillary-clinton-campaign-message-keeps-evolving/BiGL9cA8Isob3ZihtwrdyK/story.html.

"Make America Great Again." Wikipedia, accessed June 30, 2020, https://en.wikipedia.org/wiki/Make_America_Great_Again.

Plous, Scott. The Psychology of Judgment and Decision Making (New York: McGraw-Hill, 1993).

Rathje, Steve. "The Power of Framing: It's Not What You Say, It's How You Say It." *The Guardian*, July 20, 2017, https://www.theguardian.com/science/head-quarters/2017/jul/20/the-power-of-framing-its-not-what-you-say-its-how-you-say-it.

Rosen, Christopher. "Donald Trump Defends Twitter Use as 'Modern Day Presidential.'" *Entertainment Weekly*, July 1, 2017, https://ew.com/tv/2017/07/01/donald-trump-modern-day-presidential.

Rove, Karl. "The Trump Campaign Needs to Hit 'Reset.'" *The Wall Street Journal*, July 1, 2020, https://www.wsj.com/articles/the-trump-campaign-needs-to-hit-reset-11593642544.

Scherer, Michael, Josh Dawsey, and Ashley Parker. "Stung by Crises, the Brander in Chief Searches for a Reelection Message," *The Washington Post*, June 7, 2020, https://www.washingtonpost.com/politics/stung-by-crises-the-brander-in-chief-searches-for-a-reelection-message/2020/06/07/d715a39a-a737-11ea-b473-04905b1af82b_story.html.

Schroeder, Robert. "Donald Trump Spent the Least to Win Votes, Delegates." *MarketWatch*, May 4, 2016, https://www.marketwatch.com/story/donald-trump-spent-the-least-to-win-votes-delegates-2016-05-04.

Schroeder, Robert. "Trump Has Gotten Nearly $3 Billion in 'Free' Advertising." *MarketWatch*, May 6, 2016, https://www.marketwatch.com/story/trump-has-gotten-nearly-3-billion-in-free-advertising-2016-05-06.

Seib, Gerald F. "Hillary Clinton's Larger Dilemma: Play Donald Trump's Game, or Not?" *The Wall Street Journal*, September 12, 2016, https://www.wsj.com/articles/hillary-clintons-larger-dilemma-play-donald-trumps-game-or-not-1473699891.

"The Trump Referendum." *The Wall Street Journal*, June 20, 2020, https://www.wsj.com/articles/the-trump-referendum-11593127700.

Thomas, Ken, Sabrina Siddiqui, and Chad Day. "How Joe Biden Won the Election: Votes from Blue America with Few Gains in Trump World." *The Wall Street Journal*, November 8, 2020, https://www.wsj.com/articles/how-joe-biden-won-the-election-votes-from-blue-america-with-few-gains-in-trump-world-11604862528.

Whitehouse, Mark. "'Great Again' Is Trump's Magic Twitter Mantra." *Bloomberg*, August 21, 2017, https://www.bloomberg.com/opinion/articles/2017-08-21/-make-america-great-again-is-trump-s-magic-twitter-mantra.

Youell, Joy. "What Is Framing Psychology by Definition." *BetterHelp*, last modified January 28, 2021, https://www.betterhelp.com/advice/psychologists/what-is-framing-psychology-by-definition.

## CHAPTER 4

"10 Top Innovation Quotes." Wazoku.com, accessed August 11, 2015, https://web.archive.org/web/20190621004405/https://www.wazoku.com/10-top-innovation-quotes.

Agrell, Sofia, and Ssandra Dunder. "The Inc.redible Risks of Using Myths! Or How Apple Has Maintained Different." Student essay, Göteborgs Universitet, 2015, http://hdl.handle.net/2077/39443.

"Apple Launches iPad." *Apple*, January 27, 2010, https://www.apple.com/newsroom/2010/01/27Apple-Launches-iPad.

Brownlee, John. "Steve Jobs Talks The iPad's Success: Most Successful Consumer Product Ever." *Cult of Mac*, March 2, 2011, https://www.cultofmac.com/84513/steve-jobs-talks-the-ipads-success-most-successful-consumer-product-ever.

Bort, Julie. "The History of the Tablet, an Idea Steve Jobs Stole and Turned into a Game-Changer." *Business Insider*, June 2, 2013, https://www.businessinsider.com/history-of-the-tablet-2013-5.

Calio, Vince, Thomas C. Frohlich, and Alexander E.M. Hess. "10 Best-Selling Products of All Time." *USA Today*, May 18, 2014, https://www.usatoday.com/story/money/business/2014/05/18/24-7-wall-st-the-best-selling-products-of-all-time/9223465.

Calio, Vince, Thomas C. Frohlich, and Alexander E.M. Hess, "These Are the 10 Best-Selling Products of All Time." *Time*, May 8, 2014. https://time.com/92765/10-best-selling-products-ever.

Clover, Juli. "16 Years Ago Today, Apple Unveiled the Original iPod." *MacRumors*, October 23, 2017, https://www.macrumors.com/2017/10/23/ipod-unveiling-16-years-ago.

Dediu, Horace. "The Most Popular Product of All Time." *Asymco*, July 28, 2018, http://www.asymco.com/2016/07/28/most-popular-product-of-all-time.

Dediu, Horace. "The Pivot." *Asymco*, May 16, 2019, http://www.asymco.com/2019/05/16/the-pivot.

"Design is not just what it looks like and feels like. Design is how it works." BrainyQuote, accessed June 26, 2021, https://www.brainyquote.com/quotes/steve_jobs_169129.

Dormehl, Luke. "Today in Apple History: Apple Puts 1,000 Songs in Your Pocket with First-Gen iPod." *Cult of Mac*, October 23, 2020, https://www.cultofmac.com/660742/today-in-apple-history-apple-puts-1000-songs-in-your-pocket-with-first-gen-ipod.

Dormehl, Luke. "Today in Apple History: Apple Racks Up Staggering $700 Million Loss." *Cult of Mac*. March 28, 2021, https://www.cultofmac.com/473471/today-in-apple-history-worst-quarter-ever/amp.

Dormehl, Luke. "Today in Apple History: It's Time to 'Think Different.'" *Cult of Mac*, August 8, 2020, https://www.cultofmac.com/441206/today-in-apple-history-its-time-to-think-different.

Dormehl, Luke. "Today in Apple History: Steve Jobs Introduces Us to the iPad." *Cult of Mac*, January 27, 2021, https://www.cultofmac.com/464302/steve-jobs-ipad-launch.

Engst, Adam. "The Few Remaining Uses of the Word 'Macintosh.'" *TidBITS*, January 10, 2020, https://tidbits.com/2020/01/10/the-one-remaining-use-of-the-word-macintosh.

Gallo, Carmine. *The Storyteller's Secret* (London: MacMillan, 2016), 13–14.

"Game Changer Definition & Example." InvestingAnswers, https://investinganswers.com/dictionary/g/game-changer.

Hormby, Tom. "Think Different: The Ad Campaign that Restored Apple's Reputation." *Low End Mac*, August 10, 2013. https://lowendmac.com/2013/think-different-ad-campaign-restored-apples-reputation.

Jobs, Steve. "Steve Jobs' iPhone 2007 Presentation (Full Transcript)." Transcribed by S. Pangambam, SingjuPost.com, July 4, 2014. https://singjupost.com/steve-jobs-iphone-2007-presentation-full-transcript.

Jobs, Steve. "To me, marketing is about values," Launch of Apple "Think Differently" Campaign 1997. *Speakola*, https://speakola.com/corp/steve-jobs-marketing-think-differently-1997.

Kagan, Marta. "7 Public Speaking Tips from the World's Best Speakers & Presenters." HubSpot, last modified January 4, 2021, https://blog.hubspot.com/blog/tabid/6307/bid/34274/7-lessons-from-the-world-s-most-captivating-presenters-slideshare.aspx.

Langley, Chris. "History as Brand: 'Think Different' and the Future of Apple." *Medium*, November 20, 2019, https://medium.com/swlh/history-as-brand-think-different-and-the-future-of-apple-a90554fcce1c.

Lidow, Derek. "The Theranos Scandal: What Happens When You Misunderstand Steve Jobs." *Forbes*, June 18, 2018, https://www.forbes.com/sites/dereklidow/2018/06/18/the-theranos-scandal-what-happens-when-you-misunderstand-steve-jobs.

Lundin, Katie. "5 Most Successful Products Ever and What Small Businesses Can Learn from Them." *Crowdspring*, March 22, 2018, https://www.crowdspring.com/blog/successful-product-design.

Lyons, Daniel. "Why the iPad Will Change Everything."
*Newsweek*, March 25, 2010, https://www.newsweek.com/
why-ipad-will-change-everything-69615.

Maney, Kevin. "Forget Disruption—Creators Dominate Markets Now."
*Newsweek*, June 4, 2016, https://www.newsweek.com/2016/06/17/
category-companies-466343.html.

"Market Share of Personal Computer Vendors." Wikipedia,
accessed May 12, 2020, https://en.wikipedia.org/wiki/
Market_share_of_personal_computer_vendors.

Mickle, Tripp. "How Tim Cook Made Apple His Own." *The Wall Street
Journal*, August 7, 2020, https://www.wsj.com/articles/tim-cook-apple-
steve-jobs-trump-china-iphone-ipad-apps-smartphone-11596833902.

Nations, Daniel. "How Many iPads Have Been Sold?" *LifeWire*,
last modified March 3, 2021, https://www.lifewire.com/
how-many-ipads-sold-1994296.

Peers, Martin. "Apple's Hard-to-Swallow Tablet." *The Wall Street Journal*,"
December 30, 2009, https://www.wsj.com/articles/SB1000142405274870
3510304574626213985068436.

Reisinger, Don. "Apple's iPad Turns 10: Experts Look at the Decades Behind
and Ahead." *Fortune*, January 28, 2020, https://fortune.com/2020/01/28/
apple-ipad-impact-10-years-old-sales.

"Revenue of Apple from iPad Sales Worldwide from 3rd
Quarter 2010 to 4th Quarter 2020." Statista, accessed
June 26, 2021, https://www.statista.com/statistics/269914/
apples-global-revenue-from-ipad-sales-by-quarter.

Siltanen, Rob. "The Real Story Behind Apple's 'Think
Different' Campaign." *Forbes*, December 14, 2011,
https://www.forbes.com/sites/onmarketing/2011/12/14/
the-real-story-behind-apples-think-different-campaign.

Stoll, John D. "Can Design Thinking Save Business?" *The Wall
Street Journal*, January 31, 2020, https://www.wsj.com/articles/
can-design-thinking-save-business-11580484219.

Tanimoto, Craig. "08: Apple (1997)—Think Different." Creative Review, accessed June 26, 2021, https://www.creativereview.co.uk/apple-think-different-slogan.

"Think (IBM)." Wikipedia, accessed June 24, 2020, https://en.wikipedia.org/wiki/Think_(IBM).

"Think Different." Wikipedia, accessed June 22, 2020, https://en.wikipedia.org/wiki/Think_different.

Ulloa Carrasco, Aldo. "You Can't Just Ask Customers." SlideShare, June 20, 2013 https://www.slideshare.net/AldoUlloaCarrasco/03-inspirational-quotes/14-You_cant_just_ask_customers.

Vogelstein, Fred. "How Steve Jobs Made the iPad Succeed When All Other Tablets Failed." *Wired*, November 2, 2013. https://www.wired.com/2013/11/one-ipad-to-rule-them-all-all-those-who-dream-big-are-not-lost.

Winer, Dave. "Notes from a Beer-Food-Steve Party at Apple." DaveNext, last modified September 30, 1997. http://scripting.com/davenet/studies/beerFoodAndSteve.html.

Zink, Dennis. "Business alchemist: Remembering the Wisdom of Apple's Steve Jobs." *Herald-Tribune*, November 23, 2020, https://www.heraldtribune.com/story/business/briefs/2020/11/23/dennis-zink-remembering-wisdom-apples-steve-jobs/6338676002.

## CHAPTER 5

"2018 Starbucks Global Social Impact Report." Starbucks, accessed June 27, 2021, https://globalassets.starbucks.com/assets/5064028eb31b40fa86c13dd54497de1f.pdf.

*Best Global Brands 2019*. New York: Interbrand, 2019, https://www.interbrand.com/wp-content/uploads/2019/10/Interbrand_Best_Global_Brands_2019.pdf.

Campbell, Kunle. "Starbucks Red Cups Spark Consumer Salivating (and Controversy)." BigCommerce, accessed June 27, 2021, https://www.bigcommerce.com/blog/starbucks-red-cups-holiday-campaign.

"Company Information." Starbucks, accessed June 27, 2021, https://www.starbucks.com/about-us/company-information.

Dollinger, Mathew. "Starbucks, 'The Third Place', and Creating the Ultimate Customer Experience." *Fast Company*, June 8, 2008, https://www.fastcompany.com/887990/starbucks-third-place-and-creating-ultimate-customer-experience.

Eira, Astrid. "Number of Starbucks Worldwide 2020: Facts, Statistics, and Trends." FinancesOnline, accessed June 27, 2021, https://financesonline.com/number-of-starbucks-worldwide.

Gallo, Carmine. "Starbucks CEO: Lesson in Communication Skills." *Forbes*, March 25, 2011, https://www.forbes.com/sites/carminegallo/2011/03/25/starbucks-ceo-lesson-in-communication-skills.

Gallo, Carmine. *The Storyteller's Secret*. London: MacMillan, 2016, 47.

Geereddy, Nithin. *Strategic Analysis of Starbucks Corporation*. Boston: Harvard University, 2013, https://scholar.harvard.edu/files/nithingeereddy/files/starbucks_case_analysis.pdf.

"History and Background of Starbucks." MBA Knowledge Base, accessed April 20, 2013. https://www.mbaknol.com/business-history/history-and-background-of-starbucks.

Hunt, Galen. "Introducing Microsoft Azure Sphere: Secure and Power the Intelligent Edge." *Microsoft Azure*, April 16, 2018, https://azure.microsoft.com/en-us/blog/introducing-microsoft-azure-sphere-secure-and-power-the-intelligent-edge.

Hitt, Michael A., R. Duane Ireland, and Robert E. Hoskisson, *Strategic Management: Competitiveness & Globalization: Concepts and Cases*, 12th ed. Boston: Cengage Learning, 2017: C–223-236 https://bawar.net/data0/books/5ea6b715e53cf/pdf/strategic.pdf.

Michelli, Joseph. "The Starbucks Experience: 5 Principles for Turning Ordinary into Extraordinary." McGraw-Hill Education; 1 edition (October 5, 2006).

"Number of Starbucks Stores Worldwide from 2003 to 2019." Statista, accessed June 27, 2021, https://www.statista.com/statistics/266465/number-of-starbucks-stores-worldwide.

Sokolowsky, Jennifer. "Starbucks Turns to Technology to Brew Up a More Personal Connection with Its Customers." *Microsoft*, May 6, 2019, https://news.microsoft.com/transform/starbucks-turns-to-technology-to-brew-up-a-more-personal-connection-with-its-customers.

"Starbucks." Wikipedia, accessed June 29, 2020, https://en.wikipedia.org/wiki/Starbucks.

"Starbucks Company Timeline." *Starbucks*, August 6, 2015, https://web.archive.org/web/20150906183546/https://news.starbucks.com/uploads/documents/AboutUs-Timeline-Q32015-8.6.2015.pdf.

"Starbucks Corporation." Google Finance, accessed December 22, 2020, https://www.google.com/finance/quote/SBUX:NASDAQ?sa=X&ved=2ahUKEwi-5-3LxvPsAhXPCTQIHaXoB8oQ3ecFMAB6BAgBEBE.

"Starbucks Green Barista Apron." Amazon.com, https://www.amazon.com/starbucks-starbucks-green-barista-apron/dp/b00fyz9br4.

"Starbucks Takes High Road in Coffee Wars." *Chicago Tribune*, December 11, 2008, https://www.chicagotribune.com/news/ct-xpm-2008-12-11-0812110258-story.html.

"Use of the Third Place Policy." *Starbucks Stories & News*, last modified August 24, 2020, https://studies.starbucks.com/studies/2018/use-of-the-third-place-policy/.

Warnick, Jennifer. "AI for Humanity: How Starbucks Plans to Use Technology to Nurture the Human Spirit." *Starbucks Stories and News*, January 10, 2020, https://studies.starbucks.com/studies/2020/how-starbucks-plans-to-use-technology-to-nurture-the-human-spirit.

"When Do Starbucks' Christmas Drinks Return?" Countdown to #redcups, accessed June 27, 2021, https://www.countdowntoredcups.com.

White, Colin. "Starbucks: The Third Place." in *Strategic Management* (London: Palgrave, 2004), 766–72, https://doi.org/10.1007/978-0-230-55477-1_29.

Wiener-Bronner, Danielle. "Why Starbucks Needs You to Feel at Home." *CNN*, September 30, 2018, https://www.cnn.com/2018/09/30/business/starbucks-third-place/index.html.

Wojno, Rebecca. "Killing It: How Starbucks is Winning at Retention." *PostFunnel*, May 16, 2017, https://postfunnel.com/killing-it-how-starbucks-is-winning-at-retention.

Zhang, Jonathan, and Hsiao-Wuen Hon, "Embracing Digital Transformation as-a-Service." *California Review Management*, February 19, 2020, https://cmr.berkeley.edu/2020/02/digital-transformation-as-a-service.

# CHAPTER 6

Clark, Kate. "'We Are Seeing Volume and Interest in Peloton Explode,' Says Company President on Listing Day." *TechCrunch*, September 26, 2019, https://techcrunch.com/2019/09/26/peloton-goes-public.

Clark, Kate. "Peloton Files Publicly for IPO." *TechCrunch*, August 27, 2019, https://techcrunch.com/2019/08/27/peloton-files-publicly-for-ipo.

Darrah, Paige. "Success Cycle." *Hemispheres*, December 2020, 68, https://www.hemispheresmag.com/wp-content/uploads/2020/11/FULL_EDITION_v2-1.pdf.

De Silva, Matthew. "For Peloton to Succeed, It Needs to Turn Loyalty into Cash." *Quartz*, November 6, 2019, https://qz.com/1742728/peloton-doubled-its-subscribers-but-growth-is-slowing.

"Investor & Analyst Session." *Peloton*, September 15, 2020, https://investor.onepeloton.com/static-files/5155a9dc-1da8-4d6a-b232-3c231b8983b6.

Jannarone, John. "This Metric is the Key to Peloton Keeping Its Lead Over the Pack." *Yahoo! Finance*, September 26, 2019, https://finance.yahoo.com/news/metric-key-peloton-keeping-lead-180813105.html.

Roth, Daniel. "No One Believed in Peloton's CEO as He Built the Company. Here's How John Foley Just Kept Climbing." *LinkedIn*, March 13, 2019, https://www.linkedin.com/pulse/one-believed-pelotons-ceo-he-built-company-heres-how-john-daniel-roth.

Stoll, John D. "Peloton Rides Covid-19 Wave, Adding Products, Cutting Bike Price." *The Wall Street Journal*, September 8, 2020, https://www.wsj.com/articles/peloton-rides-covid-19-wave-adding-products-cutting-bike-price-11599561900.

"The Peloton Bike: Bring Home the Studio Cycling Experience." Kickstarter, November 22, 2013, https://www.kickstarter.com/projects/568069889/the-peloton-bike-bring-home-the-studio-cycling-exp.

## CHAPTER 7

"2020 Investor Presentation." *Uber*, February 6, 2020, https://s23.q4cdn.com/407969754/files/doc_financials/2019/sr/InvestorPresentation_2020_Q4.pdf.

"An Interview with the Founder of Seedlip, the World's First Non-Alcoholic Spirit." The Challenger Project, https://thechallengerproject.com/blog/2015/seedlip.

Bell, Douglas. "World's First 'Non-Alcoholic Spirit' Bought by Alcohol Giant, Diageo; A 'Game-Changing' Innovation?" *Forbes*, August 14, 2019, https://www.forbes.com/sites/douglasbell/2019/08/14/sold-the-worlds-most-expensive-soft-drink-founder-bought-out-by-global-alcohol-giant-diageo.

Belyh, Anastasia. "How to Create a Brand-new Market." *Cleverism*, last modified September 23, 2019, https://www.cleverism.com/create-brand-new-market.

Bloom, Olivia. "A Non-Alcoholic Spirit That Tastes Just Like a Craft Cocktail." *Food52*, March 20, 2017, https://food52.com/blog/19198-a-non-alcoholic-spirit-that-tastes-just-like-a-craft-cocktail.

Branson, Ben. Personal Communication, August 13, 2020.

"Diageo Acquires Majority Shareholding in Seedlip, the World's First Distilled Non-Alcoholic Spirit." Diageo, August 7, 2019, https://www.diageo.com/en/news-and-media/features/diageo-acquires-majority-shareholding-in-seedlip-the-world-s-first-distilled-non-alcoholic-spirit.

Fleming, Molly. "The World's First Distilled Non-Alcoholic Spirit Has 'Pioneered' the Category, but as Competition Grows It Must Remain as Agile as When It First Began." *MarketingWeek*, February 5, 2020, https://www.marketingweek.com/seedlip-no-alcohol-campaign.

French, John. *The Art of Distillation*. London: Richard Cotes, 1651, https://brbl-dl.library.yale.edu/vufind/Record/3441309.

Galbraith, Anna. "Uncorking the Extraordinary Success of Seedlip." *Gentlemen's Journal*, https://www.thegentlemansjournal.com/article/uncorking-the-extraordinary-success-of-seedlip.

Ince, John. "Why Did Sidecar Fail?" *Ride Share Guy*, February 10, 2016, https://therideshareguy.com/why-did-sidecar-fail.

Magee, Kate. "How Seedlip and Diageo Created a Successful Booze-Free Spirit." *CampaignLive*, June 6, 2017, https://www.campaignlive.com/article/seedlip-diageo-created-successful-booze-free-spirit/1435639.

Meah, Josh. "Uber Marketing Strategy: 15 Takeaways for Entrepreneurs." *Josh Meah & Company*, May 15, 2019, https://www.joshmeah.com/15-lessons-from-ubers-marketing-strategy.

Miller, Grace. "Uber's Marketing Strategy In 7 Steps, Revisited." Annex Cloud, https://www.annexcloud.com/blog/ubers-marketing-strategy-in-7-steps-revisited.

Parker, Melissa. "Seedlip Founder Reveals What's Next in the No-Alcohol Market." *Drinks Trade*, August 6, 2019, https://www.drinkstrade.com.au/seedlip-founder-reveals-whats-next-in-the-no-alcohol-market.

Pathak, Puranjan. "A Study on Business Model Adopted by UBER to Disrupt the Taxi Industry." *International Journal of Scientific & Engineering Research* 8, no. 8 (August-2017), https://www.ijser.org/researchpaper/A-study-on-Business-model-adopted-by-UBER-to-disrupt-the-Taxi-Industry.pdf.

Perea, Christian. "RIP Sidecar: Company Will Cease Rideshare and Delivery Services." *Ride Share Guy*, December 29, 2015. https://therideshareguy.com/rip-sidecar-company-will-cease-rideshare-and-delivery-services.

Said, Carolyn. "Ride-Sharing Pioneer Sidecar to Shut Down Ride, Delivery Service." *SF Gate*, December 29, 2015, https://www.sfgate.com/business/article/Ride-sharing-pioneer-Sidecar-to-shut-down-ride-6726144.php.

Singh, Spandana. "Dating Apps Are Even Less Transparent Than Facebook and Google." *Slate*, February 13, 2021, https://slate.com/technology/2021/02/dating-apps-content-moderation-transparency-policies.html.

"The Roots of Seedlip." Seedlip, https://www.seedlipdrinks.com/en-us/our-story.

"Uber Technology Offerings." Uber, https://www.uber.com/us/en/about/uber-offerings.

Yoon, Eddie, and Linda Deeken. "Why It Pays to Be a Category Creator." *Harvard Business Review*, March 2013, https://hbr.org/2013/03/why-it-pays-to-be-a-category-creator.

## CHAPTER 8

Adam, Karla. "'Get Brexit Done': Boris Johnson's Effective but Misleading Slogan in the British Election." *The Washington Post*, December 19, 2019, https://www.washingtonpost.com/world/europe/get-brexit-done-boris-johnsons-effective-but-misleading-slogan-in-the-uk-election/2019/12/12/ec926baa-1c62-11ea-977a-15a6710ed6da_story.html.

Bella, Timothy. "'Just Do It': The Surprising and Morbid Origin Story of Nike's Slogan." *The Washington Post*, September 4, 2018, https://www.washingtonpost.com/news/morning-mix/wp/2018/09/04/from-lets-do-it-to-just-do-it-how-nike-adapted-gary-gilmores-last-words-before-execution.

Berberich, Michael. "Why Does GEICO Run So Many Different TV Ads All at Once?" *Association of National Advertisers*, January 14, 2015, https://www.ana.net/blogs/show/id/33233.

Bigelow, James, and Amy Poremba. "Achilles' Ear? Inferior Human Short-Term and Recognition Memory in the Auditory Modality." *PLoS ONE* 9, no. 2 (February 26, 2014): e89914, https://doi.org/10.1371/journal.pone.0089914.

Cowan, Nelson. Curators' Professor of Psychology at the University of Missouri, Personal Communication, September 14, 2020.

Cowan, Nelson. "The Magical Mystery Four: How is Working Memory Capacity Limited, and Why?" *Current Directions in Psychological Science* 2010 Feb 1; 19(1): 51–57.

Danise, Amy. "List of Car Insurance Companies 2020." *Forbes*, May 20, 2020, https://www.forbes.com/advisor/car-insurance/companies-list.

"Fast Facts." StateFarm, accessed April 17, 2021, https://www.statefarm.com/about-us/company-overview/company-profile/fast-facts.

"GEICO Advertising Campaigns." Wikipedia, accessed May 10, 2020, https://en.wikipedia.org/wiki/GEICO_advertising_campaigns.

GEICO Insurance, "The Gecko Reveals '15 Minutes' Origin—GEICO Insurance." YouTube video, November 1, 2020, https://www.youtube.com/watch?v=-30ONClGBd8.

"GEICO Tops List of First Quarter's Biggest Ad Spenders." *InsideRadio*, January 9, 2020, http://www.insideradio.com/geico-tops-list-of-first-quarter-s-biggest-ad-spenders/article_26e3d570-32be-11ea-aca2-6f8989fa4f36.html.

Herr, Cynthia. "Three Ingredients for a Great Ad: A Geico Analysis." HawkPartners, https://hawkpartners.com/branding/three-ingredients-for-a-great-ad-a-geico-analysis.

Kagan, Marta. "7 Public Speaking Tips from the World's Best Speakers & Presenters." *HubSpot*, last modified January 4, 2021, https://blog.hubspot.com/blog/tabid/6307/bid/34274/7-Lessons-From-the-World-s-Most-Captivating-Presenters-SlideShare.aspx.

Kessler, Martin. "The Story Behind Nike's 'Just Do It' Slogan." *WBUR*, November 23, 2018, https://www.wbur.org/onlyagame/2018/11/23/just-do-it-nike-gilmore.

Kiger, Patrick, and Andy Markowitz. "Nation's Largest Auto Insurers Refunding Policyholders." AARP, last modified July 10, 2020, https://www.aarp.org/auto/car-maintenance-safety/info-2020/coronavirus-car-insurance-premium-refund.html.

Lant, Karla, and Kelly Morr. "The History of Logos." 99Designs, accessed June 29, 2021, https://99designs.com/blog/design-history-movements/the-history-of-logos.

"Memory and Retention in Learning." Wikipedia, accessed June 8, 2020, https://en.wikipedia.org/wiki/Memory_and_retention_in_learning.

Miller, George A. "The Magical Number Seven, plus or Minus Two: Some Limits on Our Capacity for Processing Information." *Psychological Review* 63, no. 2 (1956): 81–97, https://doi.org/10.1037/h0043158.

Mohs, Richard C. "How Human Memory Works." HowStuffWorks, May 8, 2007, https://science.howstuffworks.com/life/inside-the-mind/human-brain/human-memory.htm.

Perrigo, Billy. "'Get Brexit Done.' The 3 Words That Helped Boris Johnson Win Britain's 2019 Election." *Time*, December 13, 2019, https://time.com/5749478/get-brexit-done-slogan-uk-election.

Pilcher, Jeffry. "GEICO's Crazy Ad Strategy Breaks the Rules." The Financial Brand, January 22, 2010, https://thefinancialbrand.com/9663/geico-gecko-caveman-kash-tv-commercials.

Porter, Tom. "The Winning Slogan from Every US Presidential Campaign Since 1948." *Business Insider*, May 15, 2019, https://www. businessinsider.com/every-winning-slogan-from-us-presidential-campaigns-1948-2016-2019-5.

Quinn, Renee C. "The Power of Branding Through Catchy Advertising, GEICO Commercials." *IPS Watchdog*, February 24, 2011, https://www.ipwatchdog.com/2011/02/24/the-power-of-branding-through-catchy-advertising-geico-commercials/ id=13081.

"Steve Jobs: 'There's Sanity Returnings.'" *Business Week*, May 25, 1998, https://www.bloomberg.com/news/articles/1998-05-25/ steve-jobs-theres-sanity-returning.

"Swoosh." Wikipedia, accessed July 4, 2020, https://en.wikipedia.org/wiki/ Swoosh.

White, Ron. "Memory Is Repetition and Reinforcement." Memorise, February 5, 2014, http://memorise.org/brain-articles/ memory-repetition-reinforcement.

"Why the 'Peculiar' Stands Out in Our Memory." *ScienceDaily*, June 19, 2017, https://www.sciencedaily.com/releases/2017/06/170619092713.htm.

## CHAPTER 9

Blakely, Lindsay. "How Sweetgreen Hopes to Turn Sustainable Salad into a National Movement." *Inc.*, October 2017, https://www.inc.com/ magazine/201710/lindsay-blakely/Sweetgreen-supply-chain.html.

De Silva, Pam. "How Sweetgreen Is Winning at Marketing." *Medium*, November 25, 2015, https://medium.com/@ pamdesilva/5-ways-sweetgreen-is-winning-at-marketing-1355013f5cc.

Dunn, Elizabeth G. "In a Burger World, Can Sweetgreen Scale Up?" *The New York Times*, January 4, 2020, https://www.nytimes. com/2020/01/04/business/sweetgreen-salads.html.

Galarza, Daniela. "How Sweetgreen Got to $1 Billion." *Eater*, November 15, 2018, https://www.eater.com/2018/11/15/18096104/sweetgreen-1-billion-unicorn-tech-company-lifestyle-brand.

Kramar, Andrea, and Tom Huddleston Jr. "How These 33-Year-Olds Are Taking Sweetgreen from a Dorm Room Start-Up to the 'Starbucks of Salad.'" *CNBC*, March 13, 2019, https://www.cnbc.com/2019/03/13/Sweetgreen-from-a-dorm-room-start-up-to-the-starbucks-of-salad.html.

Kwittken, Aaron. "How Sweetgreen Found Its Sweet Spot, On Purpose." *Forbes*, April 9, 2019, https://www.forbes.com/sites/aaronkwittken/2019/04/09/how-Sweetgreen-found-its-sweet-spot-on-purpose.

"What Sweetgreen Can Teach Startups About Scaling Intimacy." First Round Review, https://firstround.com/review/what-sweetgreen-can-teach-startups-about-scaling-intimacy.

Zolman, Laura. "Sweetgreen's Bold Plan to Disrupt the Delivery Business." *QSR Magazine*, September 27, 2018, https://www.qsrmagazine.com/exclusives/sweetgreens-bold-plan-disrupt-delivery-business.

## CHAPTER 10

Conlon, Jerome. "The Brand Brief Behind Nike's Just Do It Campaign." BrandingStrategyInsider, August 6, 2015, https://www.brandingstrategyinsider.com/behind-nikes-campaign.

Fairs, Marcus. "Nike's 'Just Do It' Slogan Is Based on a Murderer's Last Words, Says Dan Wieden." *Dezeen*, March 14 2015, https://www.dezeen.com/2015/03/14/nike-just-do-it-slogan-last-words-murderer-gary-gilmore-dan-wieden-kennedy.

"History of Advertising: Nike's 'Just Do It' Tagline." *Campaign*, January 22, 2015, https://www.campaignlive.co.uk/article/history-advertising-no-118-nikes-just-it-tagline/1329940.

"Just Do It." Wikipedia, accessed July 10, 2020, https://en.wikipedia.org/wiki/Just_Do_It.

McGill, Douglas C. "Nike Is Bounding Past Reebok." *The New York Times*, July 11, 1989, https://www.nytimes.com/1989/07/11/business/nike-is-bounding-past-reebok.html.

Moriello, John. "Serial Killer Gary Gilmore's Execution Inspired Nike's 'Just Do It' Slogan." *Sportscasting*, April 30, 2020, https://www.sportscasting.com/serial-killer-gary-gilmores-execution-inspired-nikes-just-do-it-slogan.

"Top 10 Biggest Sportswear Brands in the World." All Top Everything, accessed February 28, 2021, https://www.alltopeverything.com/top-10-sportswear-brands.

Wieden, Dan. "02: Nike (1987)—Just Do It," *Creative Review*, https://www.creativereview.co.uk/just-do-it-slogan.

"What is a Product Manager's Job." ProductPlan, https://www.productplan.com/from-brexit-to-bernie-what-product-managers-can-learn-from-politics.

Winer, Dave. "Notes from a Beer-Food-Steve Party at Apple." *DaveNet*, September 30, 1997, http://scripting.com/davenet/studies/beerFoodAndSteve.html.

## CHAPTER 11

"Amazon Mission Statement and Vision Statement In A Nutshell," FourWeekMBA, https://fourweekmba.com/amazon-vision-statement-mission-statement/.

"Amazon: Striving to be Earth's Most Customer-Centric Company." SiliconValleyTours, 2018; see https://www.aboutamazon.com/about-us.

Bavister, Stephen. "Customer Obsession: The Secret to Amazon's Success." *LexisClick*, May 17, 2019, https://www.lexisclick.com/blog/customer-obsession-the-secret-to-amazons-success.

"'Customer Obsession' Is Key to Amazon's Success." *Medium,*
May 9, 2019, https://medium.com/purposeful-retail/
customer-obsession-is-key-to-amazons-success-4d01e062fd72.

D'Onfro, Jillian. "Amazon's New Delivery Drone Will Start Shipping
Packages 'In A Matter of Months.'" *Forbes,* June 5, 2019, https://www.
forbes.com/sites/jilliandonfro/2019/06/05/amazon-new-delivery-
drone-remars-warehouse-robots-alexa-prediction.

Del Rey, Jason. "The Making of Amazon Prime, the Internet's
Most Successful and Devastating Membership Program." *Vox,*
May 3, 2019, https://www.vox.com/recode/2019/5/3/18511544/
amazon-prime-oral-history-jeff-bezos-one-day-shipping.

Nirpaz, Guy. "True Customer Obsession—I Agree with Jeff Bezos."
*Totango,* January 1, 2019, https://blog.totango.com/2019/01/
true-customer-obsession-is-key-jeff-i-agree.

Palmer, Annie. "Amazon Joins the Trillion-Dollar Club Again after
Knockout Earnings Report." *CNBC,* January 31, 2020, https://www.cnbc.
com/2020/01/31/amazon-amzn-reaches-1-trillion-market-cap.html.

Pettypiece, Shannon. "Amazon Passes Wal-Mart as Biggest
Retailer by Market Value." *Bloomberg,* July 24, 2015,
https://www.bloomberg.com/news/articles/2015-07-23/
amazon-surpasses-wal-mart-as-biggest-retailer-by-market-value.

"Power Play." *Merriam-Webster Online Dictionary,* accessed June 28, 2021,
https://www.merriam-webster.com/dictionary/power%20play.

Spangler, Todd. "Amazon Prime Tops 150 Million Members."
*Variety,* January 30, 2020, https://variety.com/2020/digital/news/
amazon-150-million-prime-members-1203487355.

"Talking Innovation and Entrepreneurship with Amazon
Founder and CEO, Jeff Bezos." YouTube video uploaded by
Edison Nation, April 15, 2011, https://www.youtube.com/
watch?time_continue=102&v=_KEKkVrzeU8&feature=emb_logo.

Underwood, Brent. "I Became a Best-Selling Author on Amazon in Five Minutes with Three Dollars." *Quartz*, February 9, 2017, https://qz.com/902504/how-to-become-a-best-selling-author-on-amazon-in-five-minutes-with-three-dollars.

Valdez, Julia. "Amazon Seller Metrics: Your Way to Success in 2020." *AMZ Advisors*, January 13, 2020, https://amzadvisers.com/amazon-seller-metrics-success-2020.

"What Are Amazon Customer Metrics?" *SourceMogul*, September 16, 2020, https://www.sourcemogul.com/training/strategy/what-are-the-amazon-customer-metrics.

## CHAPTER 12

"About Google, Our Culture & Company News." Google. Accessed March 8, 2021, https://about.google.

"Analysis of Zara's Marketing Plan and Strategy." *UKEssays*, January 1, 2015, https://www.ukessays.com/essays/marketing/analysis-of-zaras-marketing-plan-and-strategy-marketing-essay.php.

Bergquist, Kevin. "Google Project Promotes Public Good." *The University Record Online*, February 13, 2006. https://www.ur.umich.edu/0506/Feb13_06/02.shtml.

Chaniago, Athina Benedicta. "From Zero to Zara: The Secret of Fast Fashion." *Healy Consultants Group Blog*, June 8, 2015, https://blog.healyconsultants.com/zero-zara-secret-fast-fashion.

Danziger, Pamela N. "Why Zara Succeeds: It Focuses on Pulling People In, Not Pushing Product Out." *Forbes*, April 23, 2018, https://www.forbes.com/sites/pamdanziger/2018/04/23/zaras-difference-pull-people-in-not-push-product-out.

"Fast Fashion." Wikipedia, accessed July 6, 2020, https://en.wikipedia.org/wiki/Fast_fashion.

Hansen, Suzy. "How Zara Grew into the World's Largest Fashion Retailer." *The New York Times Magazine*, November 9, 2012, https://www.nytimes.com/2012/11/11/magazine/how-zara-grew-into-the-worlds-largest-fashion-retailer.html.

Jhamb, Riitu. "Case Study Zara," *SlideShare*, July 20, 2013. https://www.slideshare.net/rainajhamb/case-study-zara.

Marshall, Matt. "Google's Move to 'Universal Search.'" *VentureBeat*, May 16, 2007, https://venturebeat.com/2007/05/16/googles-move-to-universal-search.

Moorehead, Liz. "What Are the 4 Ps of Marketing and the Marketing Mix?" *IMPACT*, October 7, 2019, https://www.impactbnd.com/blog/what-are-4-ps-of-marketing-mix.

"Number of Followers of Inditex's Zara in 2018, by Social Network." Statista, accessed June 29, 2021, https://www.statista.com/statistics/762313/worldwide-number-of-followers-of-zara-on-social-networks.

Page, Larry, and Sergey Brin. "2004 Founders' IPO Letter From the S-1 Registration Statement." *Alphabet Investor Relations*, accessed June 29, 2021, https://abc.xyz/investor/founders-letters/2004-ipo-letter.

Quach, Katyanna. "Whoa! Google to Power Amazon's Internet. Wait, oh, Not that Amazon. The Other One. The Rainforest." *The Register*, November 22, 2019, https://www.theregister.com/2019/11/22/loon_mobile_internet_access.

Somers, James. "Torching the Modern-Day Library of Alexandria." *The Atlantic*, April 20, 2017, https://www.theatlantic.com/technology/archive/2017/04/the-tragedy-of-google-books/523320.

Sullivan, Danny. "Google Launches 'Universal Search' & Blended Results." Search Engine Land, https://searchengineland.com/google-20-google-universal-search-11232.

Szajna-Hopgood, Ava. "Google Will Connect the Amazon Rainforest to Wireless Internet via Giant Balloons." *Charged Retail Tech News*, November 22, 2019, https://www.chargedretail.co.uk/2019/11/22/ google-will-connect-the-amazon-rainforest-to-wireless-internet-via-giant-balloons.

Twin, Alexandra. "The 4 Ps." Investopedia, last modified February 19, 2021, https://www.investopedia.com/terms/f/four-ps.asp.

Vise, David A., and Mark Malseed. *The Google Story*. Updated Edition. New York: Bantam Books, 2018: 3, 7–8.

"Zara: Disrupting the Traditional Cycle of Fashion." *Harvard Business School*, December 6, 2015, https://digital.hbs.edu/platform-rctom/ submission/zara-disrupting-the-traditional-cycle-of-fashion.

## CHAPTER 13

"About Tesla: Tesla's Mission Is to Accelerate the World's Transition to Sustainable Energy." Tesla, 2020, https://www.tesla.com/about.

Alvarez, Simon. "Tesla Model 3 Sales Are Lowering the Average Price of Electric Cars in the US." *Teslarati*, August 28, 2019, https://www. teslarati.com/tesla-model-3-sales-lowers-average-ev-prices-usa.

Artemova, Tatyana. "66 Elon Musk Quotes on Innovation and Success In Business." *IStartHub*, June 24, 2021, https://istarthub.net/51-elon-musk-business-quotes-on-innovation-and-success-in-business.

Bhasin, Hitesh. "Marketing Strategy of Tesla." *Marketing91*, May 29, 2019, https://www.marketing91.com/marketing-strategy-of-tesla.

Bursztynsky, Jessica. "Tesla Closes Day as Fifth Most Valuable U.S. Company, Passing Facebook." *CNBC*, January 8, 2021, https://www. cnbc.com/2021/01/07/tesla-passes-facebook-to-become-fifth-most-valuable-us-company.html.

"Can Tesla Maintain its Momentum?" *Knowledge@Wharton*,
August 24, 2020, https://knowledge.wharton.upenn.edu/article/
can-tesla-maintain-its-momentum.

Chain, Philippe, and Frederick Filloux, "How Tesla
Cracked the Code of Automobile Innovation."
*Monday Note*, July 12, 2020, https://mondaynote.com/
how-the-tesla-way-keeps-it-ahead-of-the-pack-358db5d52add.

*Comprehensive Dictionary of Electrical Engineering*, ed. Phillip A. Laplante.
Boca Raton, FL: CRS Press LLC, 1999.

Eisler, Matthew N. "A Tesla in Every Garage? Not So Fast." *IEEE Spectrum*,
January 28, 2016, https://spectrum.ieee.org/transportation/advanced-
cars/a-tesla-in-every-garage-not-so-fast.amp.html.

"Elon Musk Quotes." BrainyQuote, accessed June 28, 2021, https://www.
brainyquote.com/authors/elon-musk-quotes.

Foldy, Ben. "These 11 EV Startups Are Chasing Tesla.
They Can't All Win." *The Wall Street Journal*,
November 20, 2020, https://www.wsj.com/articles/
these-11-ev-startups-are-chasing-tesla-they-cant-all-win-11605884422.

Fox, Eva. "Tesla Topped 1st Place in Consumer Reports
Owner Satisfaction Survey." *Tesmanian*, March 10, 2020,
https://www.tesmanian.com/blogs/tesmanian-blog/
tesla-topped-1st-place-in-consumer-reports-owner-satisfaction-survey.

Fox, Gary. "Tesla Business Model: It's Just Different Right!" *Gary Fox*, April
5, 2020, https://www.garyfox.co/tesla-business-model.

Gurdus, Lizzy. "Tesla Is Joining the S&P 500. What Cramer and Five
Others See Ahead for the Electric-Auto Maker." *CNBC*, November 17,
2020, https://www.cnbc.com/2020/11/17/tesla-is-joining-the-sp-500-
what-cramer-and-others-see-ahead.html.

Higgins, Tim. "Tesla is J.D. Power's Top Car for Appeal after Finishing Last
in Quality." *The Wall Street Journal*, July 22, 2020, https://www.wsj.com/
articles/tesla-is-j-d-powers-top-car-for-appeal-after-finishing-last-in-
quality-11595433600.

"History of Tesla." Wikipedia, accessed July 1, 2020, https://en.wikipedia. org/wiki/History_of_Tesla,_Inc.

Jaynes, Nick. "Tesla Unveils the Model 3, Its Mass-Market Electric Car." *Mashable*, March 31, 2016, https://mashable.com/2016/03/31/ tesla-model-3-unveil.

Kapoor, Rahul. "This Will Determine Tesla's Growth Over the Next Decade." CNN Business *Perspectives*, July 29, 2020, https://www.cnn. com/2020/07/29/perspectives/tesla-competition-elon-musk-leadership/ index.html.

Kim, Larry. "50 Innovation and Success Quotes from SpaceX Founder Elon Musk." *Inc.*, March 8, 2016, https://www.inc.com/larry-kim/50-innovation-amp;-success-quotes-from-spacex-founder-elon-musk. html.

Korn, Morgan. "The Hottest Car at the New York Auto Show is a 2-Door Electric Concept." *ABC News*, April 18, 2019, https://abcnews. go.com/US/hottest-car-york-auto-show-door-electric-concept/ story?id=62480309.

Korosec, Kirsten. "Tesla Promises up to 30% Lower Rates with New Car Insurance Play." *TechCrunch*, August 28, 2019, https://techcrunch.com/2019/08/28/ tesla-promises-up-to-30-lower-rates-with-new-car-insurance-play.

Lekach, Sasha. "Why Tesla Inspires Such Devoted Stans." *Mashable*, November 12, 2019, https://mashable.com/article/ tesla-electric-car-stans-fans.

Levy, Yonatan. "The Genius of Tesla's Product Launch Strategy." *Medium*, January 4, 2018, https://medium.com/delivering-innovation/ the-genius-of-teslas-product-launch-strategy-a56e71dc5390.

Lin, Kelly. "2021 Ford F-150 vs. Chevy Silverado 1500, Ram 1500: How the Big Three Compare." *MotorTrend*, September 29, 2020, https://www. motortrend.com/news/2021-ford-f-150-vs-ram-chevrolet-1500-pickup-trucks-specs-details.

Ludlow, Edward. "Tesla's Model S Plaid Is Fastest-Accelerating Production Car." *Bloomberg*, January 27, 2021, https://www.bloomberg.com/news/articles/2021-01-27/tesla-says-model-s-plaid-is-fastest-accelerating-production-car.

Matousek, Mark. "Almost Every Single One of the 5,000 Tesla Model 3 Owners Surveyed by Bloomberg Said They Would Buy the Car Again." *Business Insider*, November 13, 2019, https://www.businessinsider.com/tesla-model-3-customers-say-they-would-buy-it-again-2019-11.

"Model S Long Range Plus: Building the First 400-Mile Electric Vehicle." Tesla, June 15, 2020, https://www.tesla.com/blog/model-s-long-range-plus-building-first-400-mile-electric-vehicle.

Musk, Elon. "The Mission of Tesla." Tesla, November 18, 2013, https://www.tesla.com/blog/mission-tesla.

"Quotes by Elon Musk." Quotation Quotes, accessed December 24, 2020, https://quotationquotes.com/quotes-by-elon-musk.

Ramsey, Mike. "Tesla Motors Says Reservations for Model 3 Surpass 276,000." *The Wall Street Journal*, April 3, 2016, https://www.wsj.com/articles/tesla-motors-says-reservations-for-model-3-surpass-276-000-1459724101.

Rowland, Christine. "Tesla, Inc.'s Mission Statement & Vision Statement (An Analysis)." *Panmore*, August 27, 2018, http://panmore.com/tesla-motors-inc-vision-statement-mission-statement-analysis.

Santilli, Peter. "Tesla Stock Joins the S&P 500: A Game Changer." *The Wall Street Journal*, December 21, 2020, https://www.wsj.com/graphics/tesla-stock-joins-the-sp500.

Schmitt, Bertell. "Tesla's Unbelievable Model 3 Pre-Order Mirage: Be Careful What You Wish For." *Forbes*, April 6, 2016, https://www.forbes.com/sites/bertelschmitt/2016/04/06/teslas-unbelievable-model-3-pre-order-mirage-be-careful-what-you-wish-for.

Stevenson, Reed. "Tesla Overtakes Toyota as the World's Most Valuable Automaker." *Bloomberg*, July 1, 2020, https://www.bloomberg.com/news/articles/2020-07-01/tesla-overtakes-toyota-as-the-world-s-most-valuable-automaker.

"Tesla, Inc." Popular Timelines, accessed December 24, 2020, https://populartimelines.com/timeline/Tesla-Inc.

"Tesla, Inc." Wikipedia, accessed July 13, 2020, https://en.wikipedia.org/wiki/Tesla,_Inc.

"The 25 Best Inventions of 2017." *Time*, December 1, 2017, https://time.com/5023212/best-inventions-of-2017.

"Tesla Model S Achieves Best Safety Rating of Any Car Ever Tested." Tesla, August 19, 2013. https://www.tesla.com/blog/tesla-model-s-achieves-best-safety-rating-any-car-ever-tested.

"The History of Tesla." Luxury Car Prints, accessed December 24, 2020, https://web.archive.org/web/20191010044051/https://www.luxurycarprints.com/the-history-of-tesla-2/.

Wayland, Michael, and Lora Kolodny, "Tesla's Market Cap Tops the 9 Largest Automakers Combined—Experts Disagree about if that Can Last." *CNBC*, December 14, 2020, https://www.cnbc.com/2020/12/14/tesla-valuation-more-than-nine-largest-carmakers-combined-why.html.

Weinberger, Matt. "The Incredible Story of Elon Musk: From Getting Bullied in School to the Most Interesting Man in Tech." *The Independent*, September 16, 2017, https://www.independent.co.uk/life-style/elon-musk-spacex-tesla-a7950601.html.

## CHAPTER 14

Alter, Charlotte. "The Budding Beauty Mogul: Emily Weiss, United States." *Time*, March 2, 2017, https://time.com/collection-post/4684906/emily-weiss-next-generation-leaders.

"Amazon Succeeds Through Focus on Customer Over
Competitor." Insider.com. https://www.insider.com/
amazon-jeff-bezos-success-customer-obsession-2018-9.

Anderson, Will. "Journal Profile: How Curtis Eggemeyer Went from
a Salesman to CEO of a Multimillion-Dollar Cleaning Products
Business." *Biz Journals*, May 30, 2013, https://www.bizjournals.com/
austin/news/2018/05/30/journal-profile-how-curtis-eggemeyer-went-
from-a.html.

"Austin Cleaning Products Startups See Huge Surge in Sales From the
COVID-19 Pandemic." *Silicon Hills News*, April 22, 2020, http://
siliconhillsnews.com/2020/04/22/austin-cleaning-products-startups-
see-huge-surge-in-demand-from-the-covid-19-pandemic.

Branch, Kate. "Emily Weiss on What a Glossier Girl Smells Like and
Building a Cool Girl Empire." *Vogue*, September 15, 2017, https://www.
vogue.com/article/glossier-emily-weiss-global-london-paris-new-york-
body-hero-glossier-you.

"Breaking Through in a Low Interest Category." The 4A's, https://www.
aaaa.org/index.php?checkfileaccess=/wp-content/uploads/legacy-pdfs/
McGarrahJessee_LemiShine_HM.pdf.

Chitrakorn, Kati. "Build the Customer into Your Brand, Says
Glossier's Emily Weiss." *Business of Fashion*, December 1,
2017, https://www.businessoffashion.com/articles/video/
build-the-customer-into-your-brand-says-glossiers-emily-weiss.

"Clean Freaks Rejoice: Lemi Shine Introduces New Products." *CISION
PR Newswire*, February 15, 2017, https://www.prnewswire.com/
news-releases/clean-freaks-rejoice-lemi-shine-introduces-new-
products-300407575.html.

Danzige, Pamela N. "5 Reasons That Glossier Is So Successful."
*Forbes*, November 7, 2018, https://www.forbes.com/sites/
pamdanziger/2018/11/07/5-keys-to-beauty-brand-glossiers-success.

Del Valle, Gabby. "Treating Regular People like Influencers Is the Key to Glossier's Success." *Vox*, January 15, 2019, https://www.vox.com/the-goods/2019/1/15/18184151/glossier-emily-weiss-marketing-strategy-recode.

Dewey, Caitlin. "Inside the Peloverse." *Elle*, March 16, 2021, https://www.elle.com/culture/a35741771/inside-the-peloton-peloverse.

Glossier. Accessed June 30, 2021, https://www.glossier.com.

"Glossier CEO Emily Weiss on Recode Decode with Kara Swisher at the 92nd Street." YouTube video, January 14, 2019, https://www.youtube.com/watch?time_continue=327&v=Ud7cuULtfrw&feature=emb_title.

Henshall, Adam. "How a Silicon Valley Campaign Strategy Won Trump the Election." Process.st, January 27, 2017, http://www.process.st/campaign-strategy.

"How Glossier Turned Into a $400 Million Business in Four Years." *Product Habits Blog*, accessed March 12, 2012. https://producthabits.com/how-glossier-turned-into-a-400-million-business-in-four-years.

Johnson, Eric. "Full Q&A: Glossier CEO Emily Weiss on the 'Art and Science' of the Beauty Business." *Vox*, January 16, 2019. https://www.vox.com/podcasts/2019/1/16/18185512/glossier-ceo-emily-weiss-beauty-makeup-interview-podcast-recode-decode-kara-swisher.

Melzter, Marisa. "How Emily Weiss's Glossier Grew from Millennial Catnip to Billion-Dollar Juggernaut." *Vanity Fair*, October 10, 2019, https://www.vanityfair.com/style/2019/10/how-emily-weiss-grew-glossier-from-millennial-catnip-to-billion-dollar-juggernaut.

"Mission Statement." Wikipedia, accessed February 2, 2020, https://en.wikipedia.org/wiki/Mission_statement.

"Our Story." Lemi Shine, accessed June 30, 2021, https://lemishine.com/who-we-are.

Premack, Rachel. "Jeff Bezos Said the 'Secret Sauce' to Amazon's Success Is an 'Obsessive Compulsive Focus' on Customer over Competitor." *Insider*, September 15, 2018,

Roof, Katie, and Yuliya Chernova. "Glossier Tops Billion-
Dollar Valuation with Latest Funding." *The Wall Street
Journal*, March 19, 2019, https://www.wsj.com/articles/
glossier-tops-billion-dollar-valuation-with-latest-funding-11552993200.

Ruff, Corinne. "Glossier's customer obsession is
about stirring up conversation." *Retail Dive*,
March 21, 2018, https://www.retaildive.com/news/
glossiers-customer-obsession-is-about-stirring-up-conversation/519604.

Sjerin. "Has Anyone Used Lemi Shine with Success?"
Houzz, https://www.houzz.com/discussions/2334648/
has-anyone-used-lemi-shine-with-success.

"Success Story: Lemi Shine." *Bazaar Voice*, https://media.Bazaarvoice.com/
lemi-shine-success-story-v2.pdf.

Thomas, Jim. "Evolving how You Think about the Online Shopping
Journey for Specialty Retail Sites." *UX Collective*, April 9, 2020, https://
uxdesign.cc/building-a-more-effective-user-experience-for-consumers-
in-2020-fa80545d3ca7.

"We Analyzed 22 of the Biggest Direct-to-Consumer Success Stories to
Figure Out the Secrets to Their Growth—Here's What We Learned."
*CB Insights*, December 8, 2020, https://www.cbinsights.com/research/
direct-to-consumer-retail-strategies.

"What's in Lemi Shine?—UPDATED," *Chemistry Blog*, May 18, 2012, http://
www.chemistry-blog.com/2012/05/18/whats-in-lemi-shine.

Wischhover, Cheryl. "Glossier Is Going After New Customers with
an Army of Reps." *Racked*, July 12, 2017, https://www.racked.
com/2017/7/12/15949530/glossier-international-shipping-canada-uk.

# CHAPTER 15

Abboud, Leila. "Halo Top challenges big brands for scoop of ice-cream."
*Financial Times*, March 14, 2019, https://www.ft.com/content/
b5ffbe6e-1360-11e9-a168-d45595ad076d.

"About Role Models Not Runway Models." Role Models Not Runway Models, accessed December 24, 2020, http://rolemodelsnotrunwaymodels.com/meet-the-role-models.

Atwood, Tyler. "Designer Carrie Hammer Talks Role Models in Fashion, Plus How Our Standard of Beauty Is Slowly Changing for The Better." *Bustle*, February 10, 2015, https://www.bustle.com/articles/63374-designer-carrie-hammer-talks-role-models-in-fashion-plus-how-our-standard-of-beauty-is-slowly.

Atwood, Tyler. "This May be the Most Selfless Act of Fashion Week." *Bustle*, September 3, 2014. https://www.bustle.com/articles/37961-designer-carrie-hammer-gives-woman-prosthetic-limbs-and-a-chance-to-be-a-runway-model-at.

Borovic, Kali. "Halo Top Hair Is Now a Thing & The Looks Are Actually Gorgeous." *Bustle*, January 3, 2018, https://www.bustle.com/p/halo-top-hair-is-now-a-thing-the-looks-are-actually-gorgeous-7771600.

Borovic, Kali. "These Stylists Created Hair Looks Inspired by Halo Top and OMG: It's Delicious." *Bustle*, January 3, 2018, https://www.bustle.com/p/halo-top-hair-is-now-a-thing-the-looks-are-actually-gorgeous-7771600.

"Buzz." *Merriam-Webster Online Dictionary*, accessed June 30, 2021, https://www.merriam-webster.com/dictionary/buzz.

"Carrie Hammer." LinkedIn.com, accessed July 13, 2020, https://www.linkedin.com/in/carriehammer.

Cassidy, Anne. "The Man who Created a $2bn Ice Cream Firm in His Kitchen." *BBC News*, July 2, 2018, https://www.bbc.com/news/business-44614104.

Clifford, Catherine. "How an Ex-Lawyer Built Halo Top into an Ice Cream Sensation with $347 Million in Sales." *CNBC*, November 1, 2018, https://www.cnbc.com/2018/11/01/halo-top-beat-ben—jerrys-brings-in-hundreds-of-millions-in-sales.html.

Danao, Monique. "Halo Top Increased Sales By 2,500% With Word-of-Mouth." *Referral Candy Blog*, June 5, 2020, https://www.referralcandy.com/blog/halo-top-marketing-strategy.

Deltoro, Robin (@robindeltoro). Instagram profile, accessed July 16, 2020, https://www.instagram.com/robindeltoro.

Devon, Abelman. "Women Are Posing with Pints of Halo Top Ice Cream that Match Their Hair—and the Trend Is Sweeping the Internet." Insider.com. Originally published by *Allure Magazine*. https://www.insider.com/halo-top-ice-cream-hair-trend-2018-1.

"Halo Top Creamery is Now the Best-Selling Pint of Ice Cream in the United States." *Business Wire*, July 31, 2017, https://www.businesswire.com/news/home/20170731005214/en/Halo-Top-Creamery-Best-Selling-Pint-Ice-Cream.

Hammer, Carrie. "Today We'll Change Tomorrow." Image posted to Facebook, June 10, 2016, https://www.facebook.com/photo?fbid=10105632586722876&set=ecnf.2502994.

Hammer, Carrie. Personal Communication, November 5, 2020.

Gilliland, Nikki. "How Halo Top is challenging the ice cream market." *EConsultancy*, November 11, 2019, https://econsultancy.com/how-halo-top-is-challenging-the-ice-cream-market-social-marketing-strategy.

Halo Top, accessed April 4, 2021, http://www.halotop.com.

Lee, Hojung. "How Carrie Hammer Is Changing the Meaning of Beauty in the Fashion Industry." *Love Happens Mag*, March 25, 2019, https://www.lovehappensmag.com/blog/2019/02/25/carrie-hammer-role-models-not-runway-models.

"Meet Carrie Hammer, the Fashion Designer who Believes in Role Models, Not Runway Models." *BizJournals*, February 12, 2016, https://www.bizjournals.com/newyork/news/2016/02/12/meet-carrie-hammer-the-fashion-designer-who.html.

Plank, Elizabeth. "The 39 Most Iconic Feminist Moments of 2014." *Mic*, December 4, 2014. https://www.mic.com/articles/105102/the-39-most-iconic-feminist-moments-of-2014.

Probus, Jessica. "A Quadruple Amputee Walked the Runway At New York Fashion Week." *Buzzfeed*, March 12, 2015, https://www.buzzfeed.com/jessicaprobus/a-quadruple-amputee-walked-the-runway-at-new-york-fashion-we.

Snow, Shane. "What It's Like to Eat Nothing but This Magical, Healthy Ice Cream for 10 Days." *GQ*, January 16, 2016, https://www.gq.com/story/halo-top-ice-cream-review-diet.

Spencer, Ruth. "Model Danielle Sheypuk: 'People with disabilities are consumers of fashion.'" *The Guardian*, February 14, 2014, https://www.theguardian.com/fashion/2014/feb/14/model-wheelchair-new-york-fashion-week.

"The 25 Best Inventions of 2017." *Time*, December 1, 2017, https://time.com/5023212/best-inventions-of-2017.

Vagianos, Alanna. "How One Designer Is Using 'Role Models Not Runway Models' To Empower Women." *The Huffington Post*, February 13, 2015, https://www.huffpost.com/entry/role-models-not-runway-models-carrie-hammer_n_6680742.

Whitcraft, Teri, and Jamie Zimmerman. "Karen Crespo's Triumphant Walk: How one model rocked the runway at New York Fashion Week." *ABC News*, September 8, 2014. https://abcnews.go.com/amp/Entertainment/karen-crespos-triumphant-walk/story?id=25337940.

Wohl, Jessica. "How Halo Top is Conquering the Ice Cream Biz—without Ads." *Ad Age*, March 6, 2017, https://adage.com/article/print-edition/halo-top-conquering-ice-cream-biz-ads/308177.

Yäisänen, Ida. "First model with Down syndrome in New York Fashion Week." *Seren*, February 12, 2015, https://www.seren.bangor.ac.uk/lifestyle/fashion/2015/02/12/first-model-with-down-syndrome-in-new-york-fashion-week.

# CHAPTER 16

Bezos, Jeff. "2020 Letter to Shareholders." Amazon. accessed
April 16, 2021, https://www.aboutamazon.com/news/
company-news/2020-letter-to-shareholders.

"Kennedy's Famous 'Moon' Speech Still Stirs." *Radio Free Europe Radio
Library*, September 12, 2012, https://www.rferl.org/a/kennedy-moon-
speech-rice-university-50th-anniversary/24706222.html.

Kettley, Sebastian. "JFK Moon Speech: Read President Kennedy's
Historic Rice 'We Choose to Go the Moon' Speech." *Express*,
June 19, 2019, https://www.express.co.uk/news/science/1142462/
JFK-Moon-speech-President-John-F-Kennedy-Rice-we-choose-to-go-
Moon-speech-nasa-news.

Malangone, Abigail. "We Choose to Go to the Moon: The 55th Anniversary
of the Rice University Speech." *John F. Kennedy Presidential Library and
Museum*. September 12, 2017, https://jfk.blogs.archives.gov/2017/09/12/
we-choose-to-go-to-the-moon-the-55th-anniversary-of-the-rice-
university-speech.